diy

STATEMENT NECKLACES

Create your own customizable jewelry—for less!

ERIN PRUCKNO

OF

thanks, I made it

Adams media
AVON, MASSACHUSETTS

Published by
Adams Media, a division of F+W Media, Inc.
57 Littlefield Street, Avon, MA 02322. U.S.A.
www.adamsmedia.com

ISBN 10: 1-4405-8040-5
ISBN 13: 978-1-4405-8040-6
eISBN 10: 1-4405-8041-3
eISBN 13: 978-1-4405-8041-3

Printed in the United States of America.

10 9 8 7 6 5 4 3 2 1

Library of Congress Cataloging-in-Publication Data

Pruckno, Erin, author.
 DIY statement necklaces / Erin Pruckno of *Thanks, I Made It*.
     pages cm
 Includes index.
 ISBN 978-1-4405-8040-6 (pb) -- ISBN 1-4405-8040-5 (pb) -- ISBN 978-1-4405-8041-3 (ebook) -- ISBN 1-4405-8041-3 (ebook)
 1. Necklaces. 2. Beaded jewelry. 3. Leatherwork. 4. Jewelry making. I. Title. II. Title: Do it yourself statement necklaces.
 TT860.P78 2015
 745.594'2--dc23
                                    2014038755

Cover design by Elisabeth Lariviere.
Interior photos by Erin Pruckno and Elisabeth Lariviere.

This book is available at quantity discounts for bulk purchases.
For information, please call 1-800-289-0963.

Contents

—— INTRODUCTION ——

Whether you're in the mood for a little edgy sparkle with the Crystal Spike Necklace from Chapter 4, need the easy Tassel Pendant from Chapter 2 to layer with your favorite tops, or are looking for something to glam up a little black dress like the Gold Tube Necklace from Chapter 5, the DIY necklace projects in this book have got you covered.

Do-it-yourself statement necklaces have never been more popular—and with good reason! Jewelry is the easiest way to customize your look and update your wardrobe, and a necklace can be the centerpiece of an outfit, elevating everything from a cocktail dress to your favorite tee-and-jeans combo. When you make your own necklaces, not only can you tailor your necklaces to suit your personality and your clothes, but you can also save money, especially on some of the designer-inspired necklaces in Chapter 4. In addition, seeing a DIY statement necklace through from start to finish is a lot of fun, and a great activity to do with girlfriends or to channel your creativity. There's also nothing like the feeling of wearing something you made yourself!

In *DIY Statement Necklaces*, you will find five chapters that teach you everything you need to know about making your own statement necklaces. If you're new to jewelry-making, be sure not to skip Chapter 1, which lays the foundation for the other necklaces by introducing you to some essential techniques. Once you've learned these skills, made easy by the step-by-step photos, you can use them to create the beautiful DIY statement necklaces in the other chapters and even when trying your hand at your own projects. In the later chapters, you'll learn how to work with new techniques and materials—including chain, cord, string, and ribbon—plus you'll find new ideas to help inspire your own unique projects, such as making necklaces to accessorize your favorite outfits. To help you along the way, check out the sidebars throughout for tips, tricks, and ideas for project variations. Remember, fashion is all about developing your own individual style, so have fun customizing your DIY statement necklaces to reflect your taste and personality!

—— WHAT YOU'LL NEED ——

Each DIY statement necklace is unique, so when it comes to materials, don't feel that you have to find the exact supplies featured in these projects. Instead, consider the materials lists for each tutorial as guidelines. Jewelry should be a reflection of your personality, so change things up to use your favorite color or to suit your style. It's also important to be flexible with DIY projects: Sometimes you just can't find the right bead or the necklace simply won't work out the way you like it. Rather than getting frustrated, let these little challenges inspire you to a new solution! That said, there are materials that will make jewelry-making easier and more fun for you, so before you get started, make sure you have these basic supplies on hand:

- Beading wire
- Bead reamer or awl
- Findings, the smaller parts used to form a complete piece of jewelry, in different metals and sizes, including:
  - Jump rings in a range of sizes, such as 5mm, 7mm, and 10mm
  - Crimp beads

- Head pins and eye pins in varying lengths, such as 38mm and 50mm
- Barrel cord ends
- Clasps, such as lobster clasps in 12mm size
- Glue: a strong, viscous super glue for jewelry, such as E6000 or Dazzle-Tac
- Jewelry pliers
  - Round nose
  - Chain nose
  - Flat nose
- Masking tape for wrapping cord ends to prevent unraveling
- Ruler or measuring tape
- Scissors
- Wire cutters

Once you get started with DIY jewelry, you'll find you start to accumulate lots of odds and ends! It's helpful to buy a few affordable compartment boxes for storing your materials. Keeping organized means you'll never lose track of what supplies you have.

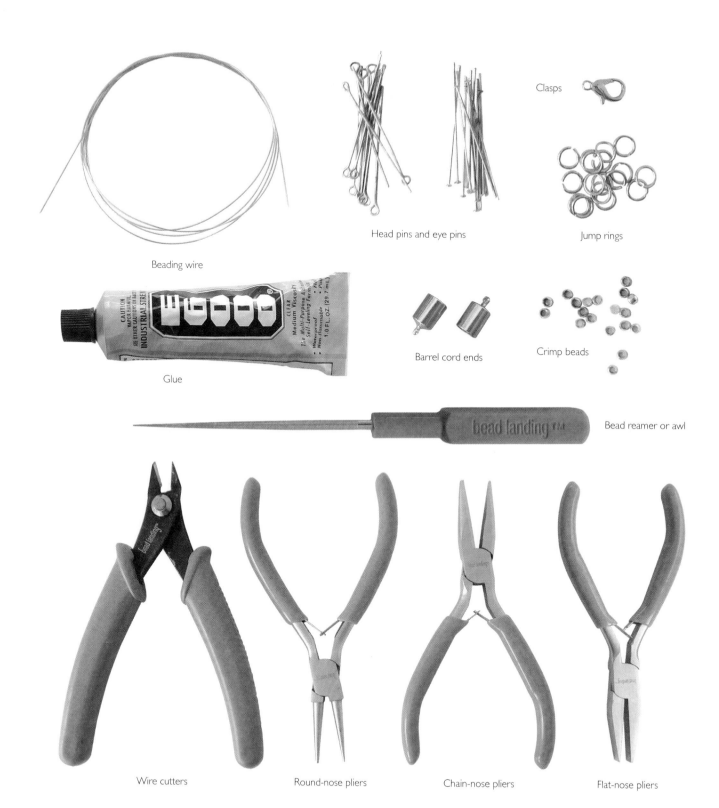

Beading wire

Head pins and eye pins

Clasps

Jump rings

Glue

Barrel cord ends

Crimp beads

bead landing™   Bead reamer or awl

Wire cutters

Round-nose pliers

Chain-nose pliers

Flat-nose pliers

Chapter 1
— BEADED STATEMENTS —

When you first start do-it-yourself jewelry-making, it's useful to begin with basic projects that will help you hone your jewelry-making skills. In this chapter, you'll learn things such as how to open and close jump rings, how to make wire loops on head pins, and how to use crimp beads. All of these skills will provide you with the basics you need to make statement necklaces of all kinds in the following chapters. These skills also get easier with practice, so if your first wire loop isn't perfectly round, don't sweat it! By the time you get to your last beads when working on a project like the Drop Bead Necklace (later in this chapter), you'll be a wire-looping pro. As you're learning, be sure to have extra findings—the smaller parts used to form a complete piece of jewelry, such as jump rings and pins—on hand so you can complete a piece without worrying about running out of supplies. And, in addition to being a great way to get started with DIY jewelry, the beaded projects in this chapter have endless options for customization, thanks to the varieties of bead materials and colors you can buy. Plastic? Semiprecious? Wood? Glass? It's up to you! Personalization is the best part about DIY.

GREEN
ASYMMETRIC
necklace

When you first start DIY jewelry-making, you want to begin with easy projects that get you used to working with the materials. This incredibly simple necklace falls into that category. While the pattern of stringing on the beads is up to you, the asymmetry of this beautiful necklace keeps it feeling modern and fresh. The mix of bead styles, united by a similar color scheme, creates an eclectic feel.

materials

- 16 inches of string or thin cord
- 16 inches of medium chain, cut into two pieces
- 30–40 beads in assorted sizes and shades of green (or other colors)

- 2 7mm jump rings
- Round-nose jewelry pliers
- Chain-nose jewelry pliers
- Clasp

 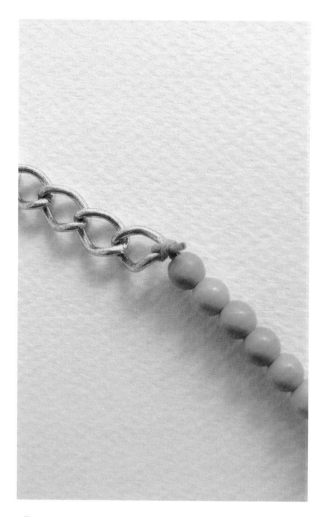

1 Tie one end of the cord or string to the end of one of the pieces of chain and string the beads on the cord. The pattern is up to you, but for an asymmetric look, string each kind of bead together in sections 2 to 4 inches long.

2 Tie the open end of the string to the end of the second chain. Trim the ends of the string.

HELPFUL HINTS

To secure the knot that you used to tie the string to the chains, add a drop of glue or clear nail polish to the knot. This will glue the string to itself, making the knot unlikely to come apart.

3 Open your jump rings by using two sets of pliers to grab on either side of the seam in the ring. Twist the pliers and ends of the jump rings away from each other in a north-south motion. Attach a jump ring to each end of the necklace, add a clasp to one side, then close each ring by twisting the ends back toward each other so the ends of the ring are flush.

HELPFUL HINTS

To make the process of opening jump rings go faster, you can invest a few dollars in a jump ring opener, a metal ring you wear on your finger with slots that allow you to insert and twist open a jump ring with just one hand.

DROP BEAD
necklace

Learning how to make wire loops on head pins or eye pins is a useful skill for working with beads. Once you've picked up the technique, this project goes quickly, and you'll breeze through all 13 beads—making the loops, connecting them, and attaching them to your necklace—in no more time than it takes to watch one of your favorite shows.

materials

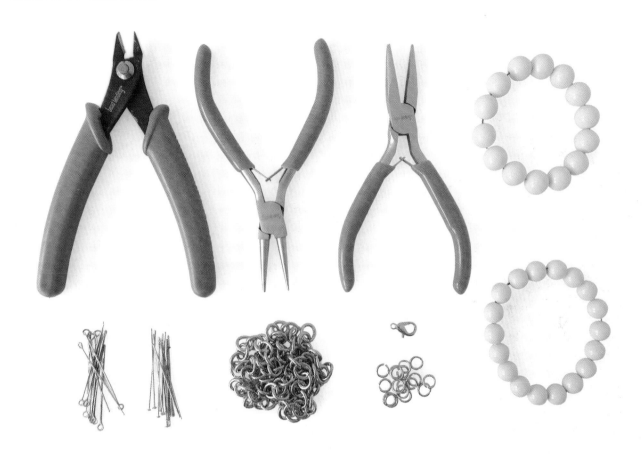

- 26 round beads, 13 medium and 13 small
- 13 head pins
- Round-nose jewelry pliers
- Chain-nose jewelry pliers
- Wire cutters

- 13 eye pins
- 13 7mm jump rings
- 18 inches of chain
- Clasp

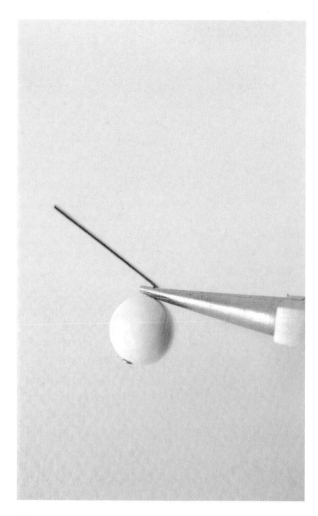

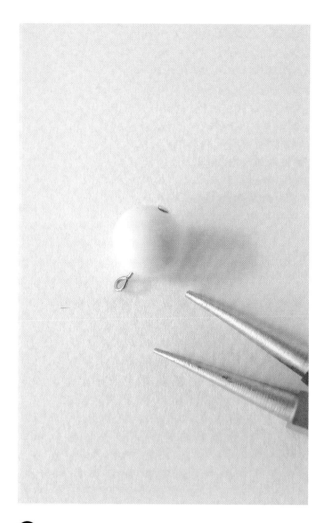

❶ Slide one of the medium-sized beads onto a head pin. Make a wire loop by grabbing the pin with the round-nose pliers, right above the bead. Use the round-nose pliers to bend the wire at a 90-degree angle. Then, use the wire cutters to clip the wire about ¼ inch from the bend.

❷ Hold the wire below the bend with the round-nose pliers. Then, grip the end of the top of the wire with the round-nose pliers and bend the wire around the round pliers until it reaches the wire at the top of the bead to form a closed loop. Repeat with the rest of the medium-sized beads.

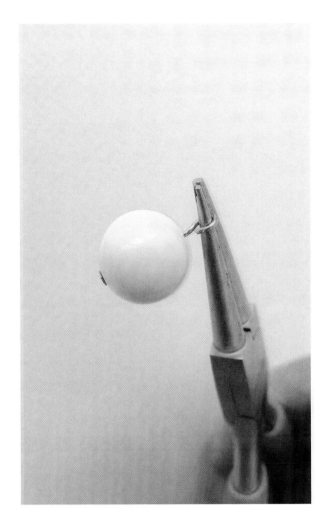

3 Next, slide a small bead on an eye pin, then repeat the wire loop technique from the medium-sized beads to form a loop at the other end of the bead. However, this time, leave the loop slightly open.

4 Connect the smaller bead to the larger by hooking the open loop of the small bead to the loop of the larger bead, and close the loop by gripping the end of the wire with the round pliers and bending it to the wire at the top of the bead. Continue to add loops to the small beads with the eye pins and connect them to the larger beads. When you're done you should have 13 sets of connected beads.

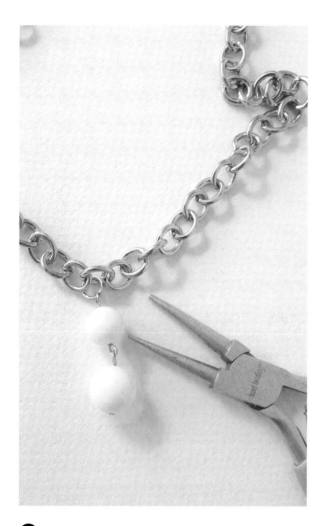

5 Take a jump ring and open it by using two sets of pliers to grab on either side of the seam in the ring. Twist the pliers and ends of the jump rings away from each other in a north-south motion. Attach one of the sets of beads to the center of the chain with the open jump ring, then close each ring by twisting the ends back toward each other so the ends of the ring are flush.

6 Add the rest of the beads to the chain, making sure to space them evenly.

●●● Make It Yours! ●●●

You don't have to stick to a monochrome palette with this necklace! Try the smaller beads in one color, and the larger beads in a complementary shade for a colorful look.

7 Attach a jump ring to each end of the chain, add a clasp to one side, then close each ring by twisting the ends back toward each other so the ends of the ring are flush.

HELPFUL HINTS

When opening jump rings, it's important to twist the ends of the rings apart in the north-south motion rather than pulling them apart east-west, which in jump rings weakens the wire, making for a less secure necklace. To close, twist the ends of the ring back toward each other.

NEON QUARTZ *necklace*

Summer's sunny days are the best time to break out the neon colors, as well as adopt easy-going bohemian styles. This necklace gives you the best of both in a modern boho statement necklace that's as easy to wear as it is to make. Once you learn how to flatten and close a crimp bead—an important but straightforward technique to master—simply slide the beads onto the beading wire.

materials

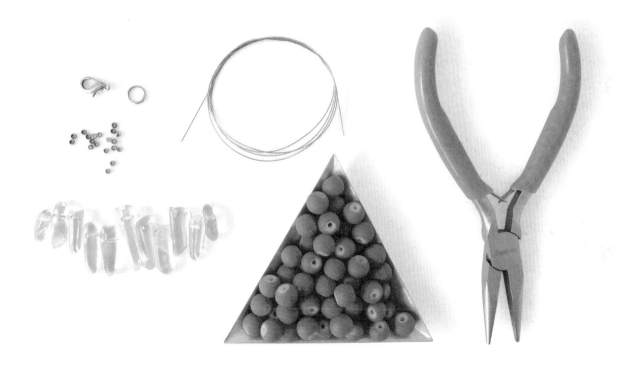

- 12 crimp beads
- Clasp
- 24 inches of beading wire
- Round-nose jewelry pliers

- Chain-nose jewelry pliers
- 58 small (8mm) round beads
- 11 quartz point beads in varying lengths
- 2 7mm jump rings

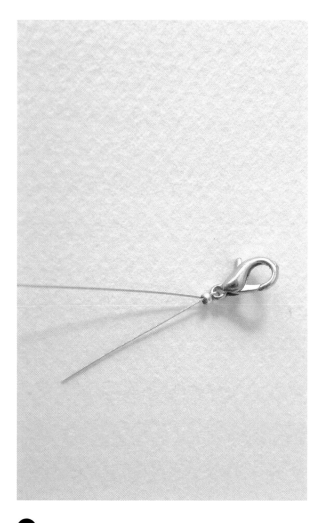

❶ Slide both a crimp bead and the loop of the clasp onto the beading wire.

❷ Fold the wire down and back through the crimp bead, forming a loop. Slide the crimp bead toward the clasp to tighten the loop.

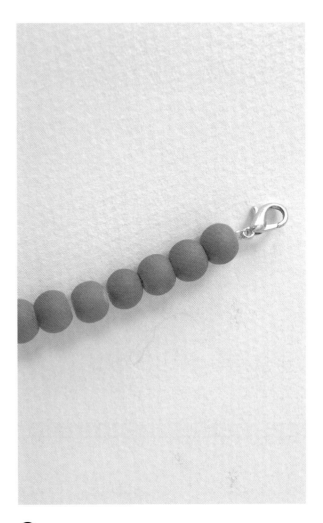

3 Using the pliers, flatten the crimp bead, pressing tightly. The squished crimp bead will prevent the wire from coming undone.

4 Thread half of the small round beads onto the wire.

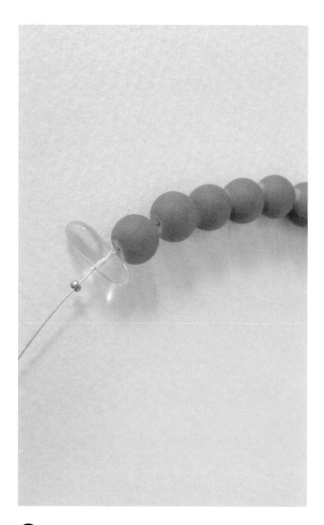

5 Slide the smallest of the quartz point beads onto the wire, followed by a crimp bead. Leave the crimp bead unflattened, so it acts as a spacer between the quartz points.

6 Continue to add the quartz beads, alternating with the tiny crimp beads. As you move toward the center, gradually add bigger quartz beads. After the longest quartz bead, add smaller points to create the graduated look. Once all the quartz beads have been added, thread the remaining round beads onto the wire.

7 Thread the wire through a crimp bead and then through a closed jump ring. Then, as you did to secure the clasp, fold the wire down and back through the crimp bead, forming a loop. Slide the crimp bead toward the clasp to tighten the loop. Secure the jump ring by flattening the crimp bead, and trim any excess wire.

STATEMENT NECKLACE SUPPLIES

While the quartz beads have a great natural look, you can buy other varieties of graduated beads in different semiprecious stones. Look online or in bead stores for fan beads (sometimes called fan pendant beads or fan stick beads) to get the flared triangle shape.

BEADED
HARDWARE
necklace

The copper couplings used in this necklace come from the plumbing section of the hardware store. They come in a range of sizes and put a fun spin on repurposed jewelry-making. They're similar in color to on-trend rose gold, but easier to find and without the designer price tag. With a subtly industrial touch, you can surprise all the friends asking where you got your unique necklace when you explain that some of the beads are actually from the hardware store! In this project, you'll learn how easy it is to make a necklace with cord. Add a fun combination of beads, knot in place, and you're on your way!

materials

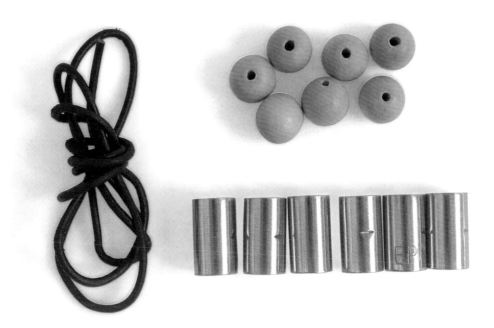

- 30 inches of cord
- 7 12mm round beads
- 6 ¼-inch copper couplings
- Scissors

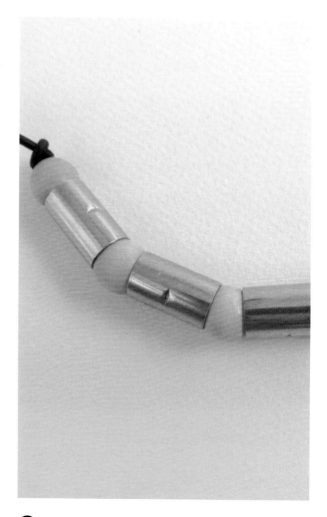

① Tie a knot in the cord about 10 inches from one end. Slide the first round bead onto the long end of the cord.

② String on the copper couplings, alternating them with beads.

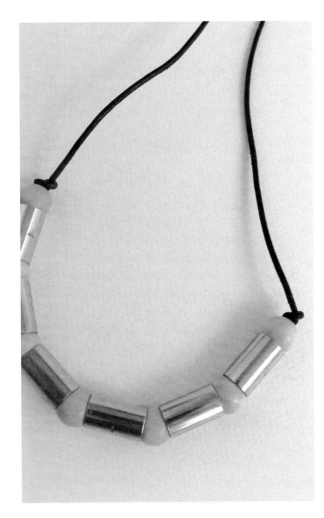

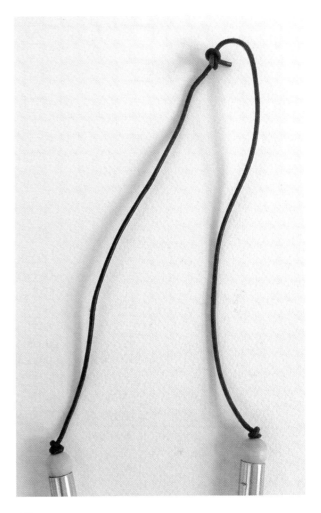

③ Once you've added enough beads, tie a second knot in the cord to secure them in place.

④ Trim the cord so the ends are even lengths. To wear, simply tie the cord in a knot behind your neck.

HELPFUL HINTS

Because copper oxidizes over time, store this necklace in a zip-top bag to reduce tarnishing. You can also try a homemade cleaner using lemon juice and salt to keep the copper bright!

BEADED RIBBON *necklace*

Play with textures by combining wood beads, metal chain, and satin ribbon in this necklace, which has a mix of materials that gives off a crafty vibe. To help slide the ribbon through the beads (which is made easier when you choose beads with large holes for stringing), push it through with a bead reamer. You can also use an awl, a skewer, or a thin but sturdy piece of wire to do the trick.

materials

- Bead reamer or awl
- 4 feet of 1-inch-wide satin ribbon
- 5 large wood beads
- 16 inches of 8mm or larger curb chain, cut into two 8-inch pieces

- 2 7mm jump rings
- Chain-nose jewelry pliers
- Flat-nose jewelry pliers
- Clasp

1 Begin by using the bead reamer to push the ribbon through your first bead. To protect the ribbon from the reamer, wrap the tip of the bead reamer with a small piece of masking tape. Insert the end of the ribbon into the bead, then continue to push all the way through with the tip of the bead reamer. Once the ribbon has reached the other side of the bead, hold onto the ribbon with your fingers and pull the bead reamer back out. The bead should now be able to slide along the ribbon.

2 Slide the bead about ⅔ of the way down the ribbon, and tie a knot on the long side of the ribbon, right next to the bead.

3 Slide the next bead onto the ribbon so the knot is between your first and second beads. Continue adding beads and knotting the ribbon.

4 Once all your beads have been added, thread one end of the ribbon through the last link of one of the lengths of chain, and tie a knot to keep it in place.

5 Weave the ribbon through the chain, in and out of the links. It helps to wrap the end of the ribbon with tape to make it easier to feed through the links.

6 Once at the end of the chain, tie a knot in the ribbon around the last link of the chain. Repeat the process with the second piece of chain on the other side of the necklace.

7 Trim the ribbon ends, then open your jump rings by using two sets of pliers to grab on either side of the seam in the ring. Twist the pliers and ends of the jump rings away from each other in a north-south motion. Attach a jump ring to each end of the necklace, add a clasp to one side, then close each ring by twisting the ends back toward each other so the ends of the ring are flush.

HELPFUL HINTS

Ribbon ends look neat when trimmed to an angle, such as a 45-degree slant. For ribbons such as the satin one used in this project, you can use a heat-sealing method to prevent fraying. Slowly bring an empty, warmed-up hot glue gun close to the unfinished edge until the ribbon starts to melt. Run the glue gun along the unfinished edge of the ribbon to seal, then leave the ribbon untouched until it's completely cool. Or, if you do not have a glue gun, a thin layer of fraying sealant or clear nail polish applied to the cut edge of the ribbon will prevent fraying.

COLOR-BLOCK *necklace*

Flat-faceted beads lend themselves perfectly to bold statement necklaces. These pebble-like beads made from lightweight acrylic are available from online retailers, and come in a rainbow of colors. You can achieve a bright color-block look for this necklace by mixing and matching coordinating hues, creating the perfect piece to liven up basic tops or dresses.

materials

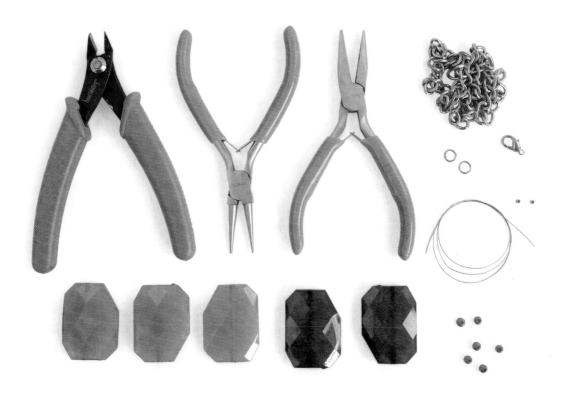

- 16 inches of beading wire or string
- 2 crimp beads
- 10 inches of chain, cut into two 5-inch pieces
- Chain-nose jewelry pliers
- Round-nose jewelry pliers

- 6 small beads
- 5 large faceted beads
- 2 7mm jump rings
- Clasp
- Wire cutters

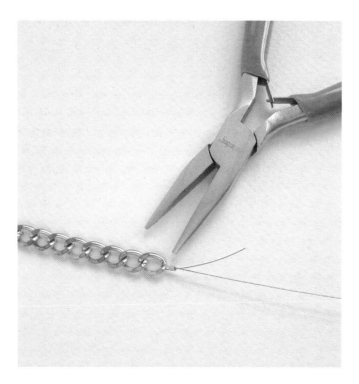

1 Slide the bead wire through a crimp bead. Loop the bead wire around the end of one of the chains, leaving about 1½ inches of wire at the short end. Fold the wire down and back through the crimp bead, forming a loop around the chain link. Slide the crimp bead over the wires toward the link and pull the end of the wire taut to tighten the loop. Secure wire in place around the jump ring by flattening the crimp bead tight around the wire. The squished crimp bead will prevent the wire from coming undone. Trim any excess from the short end of the bead wire.

2 Add a small bead to the wire, also sliding it over the short tail left behind by the crimp bead. Add the first large bead. Add the rest of the beads, alternating the small beads with the faceted ones.

HELPFUL HINTS

Once you've assembled your materials, this necklace should take you less than 15 minutes to make. Quick to put together and easy to customize, this project is a great gift for friends or family!

3 Slide a crimp bead on the wire, then loop the remaining wire around the last link of the second piece of chain. Fold the wire down and back through the crimp bead, forming a loop. Slide the crimp bead toward the clasp to tighten the loop. Using the pliers, flatten the crimp bead, pressing tightly, then trim the wire to 1 inch, and feed through the beads to conceal.

4 To complete the necklace, open your jump rings by using two sets of pliers to grab on either side of the seam in the ring. Twist the pliers and ends of the jump rings away from each other in a north-south motion. Attach a jump ring to each end of the necklace, add a clasp to one side, then close each ring by twisting the ends back toward each other so the ends of the ring are flush.

TURQUOISE SPIKE *necklace*

For a bold summer necklace, look no further than this bright Turquoise Spike Necklace to liven things up. Dyed howlite stick beads (also known as spike beads), such as those used in this project, are available online and in bead stores in a variety of candy colors that give this necklace its tropical feel. A 15-inch strand of beads in graduated sizes gives you more than enough to complete the project and leaves extras for future necklaces, such as adding some different shaped beads to the Green Asymmetric Necklace in this chapter or using the turquoise beads instead of quartz in the Neon Quartz Necklace in this chapter.

materials

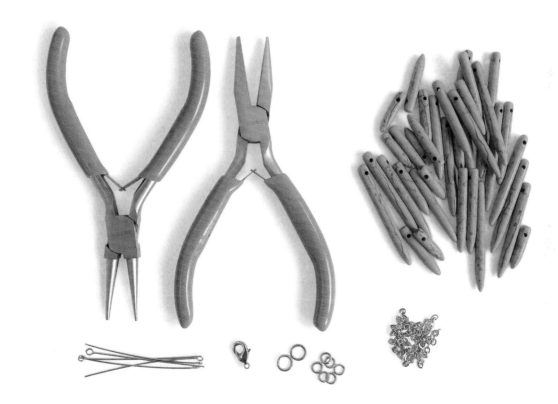

- 45 turquoise spike beads in varying sizes
- 5 50mm eye pins
- Wire cutters

- Round-nose jewelry pliers
- 6 small (5mm) jump rings
- Chain-nose jewelry pliers

- 10-inch chain, cut into two 5-inch pieces
- 2 medium (7mm) jump rings
- Clasp

① Arrange the beads into triangle sections (with the sizes moving from small to large beads and then small again), then slide them onto an eye pin.

② Trim the pin with the wire cutters, if necessary, then bend the end into a loop with the round-nose pliers.

3 Repeat four more times to create five separate triangle sections of beads.

4 Open one of the small jump rings by using two sets of pliers to grab on either side of the seam in the ring. Twist the pliers and ends of the jump ring away from each other in a north-south motion. Attach two of the triangle sections together with a small jump ring, then close the ring by twisting the ends back toward each other so the ends of the ring are flush.

5 Connect all the remaining triangles to the first two so that all five sections are connected with jump rings.

6 Add one small jump ring to each end of the necklace, connecting the loops on ends of the necklace to one of the 5–inch sections of chain.

7 Finally, attach the two medium jump rings to the end of each of the chains, adding a clasp to one side, then close the rings.

This piece uses the jewelry-making technique of making loops on eye pins. For tips on forming the loops, check out the **Drop Bead Necklace** project, also in this chapter.

Chapter 2
— CHAIN STATEMENTS —

Ranging in sizes, styles, and metals, chain is an essential material for do-it-yourself jewelry-making and is the starting point for many a great statement necklace. Many of the projects in this chapter use curb chain, which is made up of interlocking links that lie flat. Other fun types to try include rolo chain, made of wide O-shaped links; box chain, made of square links; or cable chain, made up of uniform round or oval links. In any of these projects, you can substitute your favorite color metal. You don't have to use just silver or gold, either! Copper, brass, black, and gunmetal chain along with antique finishes for gold and silver are just some of the different metals and finishes you can buy. When working with chain, be sure to match your findings to the metal of the chain so your finished piece looks polished. It's also important to make sure your findings fit, especially when working with thin chain. After picking out your chain, let it guide you as you choose findings such as jump rings that will fit through the links. Some jewelry stores sell chain by the foot, but since chain is a basic supply that's great to have on hand, stock up when you can by buying spools or in bulk.

ACRYLIC CHAIN
necklace

The chunky plastic links of acrylic chain used in this necklace put a playful spin on chain jewelry. Available online from supply vendors on sites such as Etsy, it comes in a variety of colors from classic tortoiseshell to rainbows of neons and pastels. Here, simple semi-opaque white links pop against the shiny gold of the connecting chain.

materials

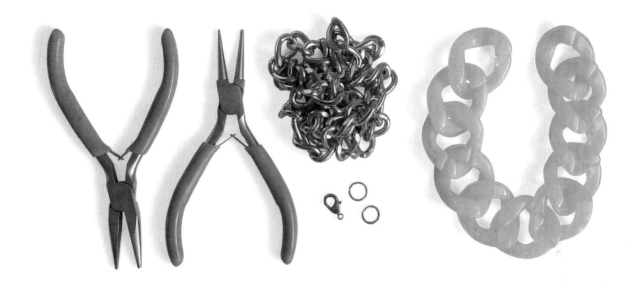

- 2 12-inch pieces of metal chain
- 10 inches of acrylic chain
- 2 jump rings

- Chain-nose jewelry pliers
- Round-nose jewelry pliers
- Clasp

1 Loop one of the gold chains through an end link of the acrylic chain. Repeat on the other side of the necklace with the other chain.

2 Open one jump ring by using two sets of pliers to grab on either side of the seam in the ring. Twist the pliers and ends of the jump rings away from each other in a north-south motion. Use the jump ring to connect the two ends of one of the gold chains, then close the jump ring by twisting the ends back toward each other so the ends of the ring are flush.

❸ Repeat on the other gold chain with the other jump ring, adding a clasp to the ring before closing the ring's ends.

••● *Make It Yours!* ●••

Since this necklace is so simple, it's easy to add your own spin. Try doubling up the acrylic chain, playing with length, or weaving a longer piece of gold chain through the larger plastic links.

TANGLED CHAIN *necklace*

While some mornings you may struggle to untangle your favorite jewelry pieces as you run out the door, the tangled chain on this necklace is essential to its elegantly undone vibe. But what's the trick for perfecting the tangled look without having to fidget with chain for hours? Easy! All you have to do is braid a few lengths of chain together, then wind the necklace with a final piece of rhinestone trim to really make this necklace stand out. This necklace would look great under the collar of a buttoned shirt, or topping off your favorite cocktail dress.

materials

- Round-nose jewelry pliers
- Chain-nose jewelry pliers
- 52 inches of 10mm curb chain, cut into one 28-inch piece and two 12-inch pieces
- 18 inches of rhinestone cup chain
- 2 rhinestone cup chain connectors, the same size as the rhinestones
- 4 jump rings
- Clasp

1 Use the pliers to open up the last link on each of the 12-inch pieces of chain.

2 Measure 8 inches in from the end of the 28-inch chain, and attach the two shorter chains by looping the open links onto the chosen link on the long chain and then closing the links with the pliers.

❸ Starting at the connected link, begin braiding the longer side of the 28-inch chain with attached 12-inch chains.

HELPFUL HINTS

It can be hard to keep your place when measuring and working with chain that slides around and looks all the same. To keep track after measuring, mark the distance by clipping a plastic bread clip around the link for an easy fix.

❹ Once you've braided to the end of the shorter chains, open the end links of the shorter chains and connect these two ends to the longer chain by looping the open links onto the chosen link on the long chain and then closing the links with the pliers.

5 Measure both ends of the necklace to ensure they are the same length. If they're uneven, shorten the longer end by opening links with your pliers to remove links until both ends are the same.

6 To attach the rhinestone chain to the necklace, first place the end of the rhinestone chain into the cup of one of the cup chain connectors and pinch it closed with the pliers. Then, open one of the jump rings by using two sets of pliers to grab on either side of the seam in the ring. Twist the pliers and ends of the jump rings away from each other in a north-south motion. Connect the jump ring to the loop of the cup chain connector and to the end of the braided part of the chain, by twisting the ends of the jump ring back toward each other so the ends of the ring are flush.

7 Wrap and loop the rhinestone chain around and through the braid, then connect it to the end of the braid with another cup connector and jump ring.

8 Add two jump rings and a clasp to the end of the necklace.

HELPFUL HINTS

Large link chains like this one are often a lightweight metal coated in a gold or silver color finish. To avoid scratching the finish with your tools, wrap the tips of your jewelry pliers with masking tape.

TASSEL
PENDANT
necklace

While collar and bib necklaces often steal the statement necklace spotlight, but it's fun to play with different necklace silhouettes to round out your wardrobe. With a long and lean silhouette, a pendant necklace like this one is an essential piece for any jewelry box. The best part of making one yourself is that you can customize its length to fit your proportions or go with your favorite outfits.

materials

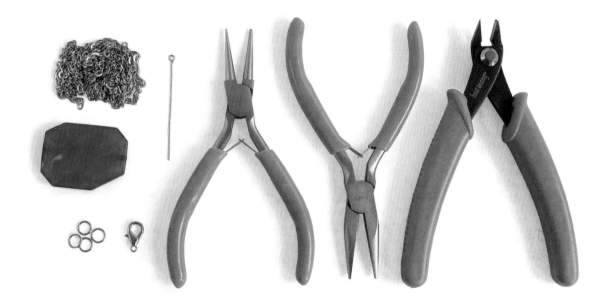

- Large bead
- 50mm eye pin
- Chain-nose jewelry pliers
- Round-nose jewelry pliers
- 4 7mm jump rings

- 38½ inches of thin chain, cut into one 26-inch piece and five 2½-inch pieces
- Wire cutters
- Clasp

❶ Slide the large bead onto the eye pin.

❷ With the pliers, bend a loop at the straight end of the eye pin by wrapping the end of the eye pin around the round nose pliers. Close the loop by bending the wire all the way around the pliers and back to the wire at the base of the bead.

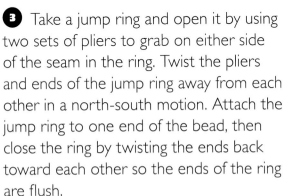 Take a jump ring and open it by using two sets of pliers to grab on either side of the seam in the ring. Twist the pliers and ends of the jump ring away from each other in a north-south motion. Attach the jump ring to one end of the bead, then close the ring by twisting the ends back toward each other so the ends of the ring are flush.

❹ Open another jump ring, and make a tassel by connecting the five smaller pieces of chain to the jump ring. To make the chains of the tassel an even length, trim with the wire cutters.

⑤ Attach the jump ring with the chains to the bottom loop of the bead.

⑥ Thread the longer 26-inch chain through the jump ring attached to the top of the bead.

7 To finish, connect two jump rings and the clasp to the ends of the long chain.

HELPFUL HINTS

The length of chain for this pendant can be flexible based on how much chain you have to work with, as well as your personal preference. You can measure a favorite necklace you already own to find a length you like, as well as try on your pendant before you add the finishing clasp, trimming the chain to fit.

ROPE AND CHAIN

Anchors away! This combination of rope and gold chain make a charmingly nautical statement necklace that pairs perfectly with striped tops or colorful shift dresses for summertime activities such as backyard barbecues or strolling along the pier. In this DIY version, a D-ring hook-and-eye closure connects the necklace, but another set of jump rings and a large lobster clasp will work as well.

materials

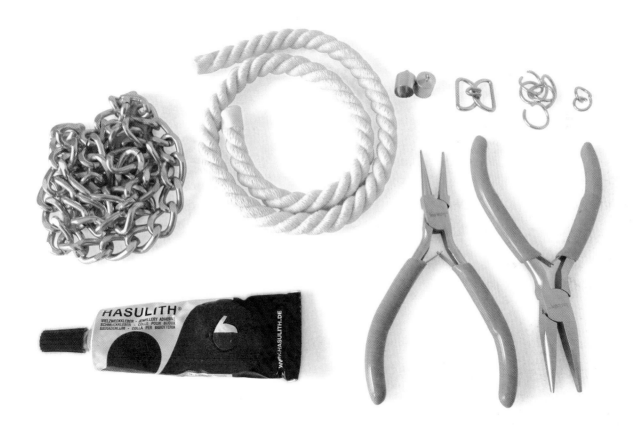

- 5 12mm jump rings
- Round-nose jewelry pliers
- Chain-nose jewelry pliers
- 21 inches of 8mm cotton rope
- 20 inches of 12mm gold curb chain

- Super glue
- 2 8mm barrel cord ends
- 2 8mm jump rings
- Large clasp or buckle

❶ Open one 12mm jump ring by using two sets of pliers to grab on either side of the seam in the ring. Twist the pliers and ends of the jump rings away from each other in a north-south motion. Once the jump ring is open, slide it onto the rope.

❷ Center the 12mm jump ring on the halfway point of the rope and the chain, then close the ring around the chain's center link by twisting the ends back toward each other so the ends of the ring are flush.

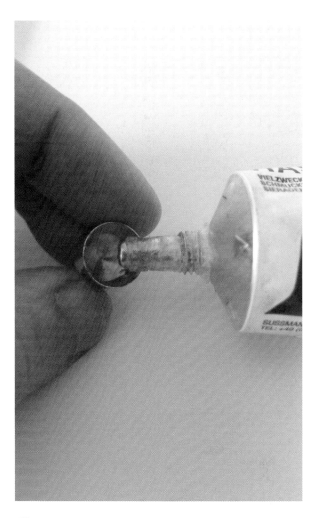

3 Open the remaining 12mm jump rings, and attach them around the rope and through the links of the chain, spacing them evenly.

4 Add a drop of glue to the barrel cord ends and press them firmly onto the ends of the rope. Let the glue dry according to package directions.

5 Use pliers to open an 8mm jump ring, and thread the ring through one barrel cord end and one side of the clasp. You can also connect the chain end to the jump ring, or you can open up the link of the chain to attach it to the closure. Close the ring, and repeat on the other end of the necklace to finish.

The length of chain is shorter than the rope by 2 inches to account for the curve of the necklace. When using the large jump rings to attach the rope and chain, remember to center the chain along the rope so there is an extra inch of rope at each end of the chain.

BOX CHAIN
necklace

Box chain gets its name from its square links that look like open boxes. With its geometric simplicity, box chain only needs a few jewels to make an elegant necklace. To cut the chain into the pieces for this project, you can use wire cutters or open up the links with pliers. Grip the top and bottom of the link with pliers in each hand, then pull the link apart.

materials

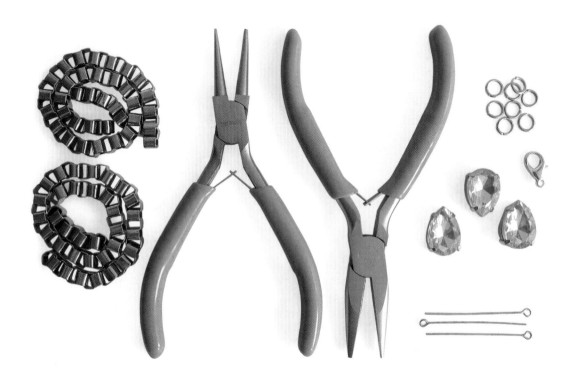

- 3 eye pins
- 3 large sew-on rhinestones in settings
- Wire cutters
- Round-nose jewelry pliers
- Chain-nose jewelry pliers

- 8 7mm jump rings
- 18 inches of box chain, cut into two 8-inch pieces and two 1-inch pieces
- Clasp

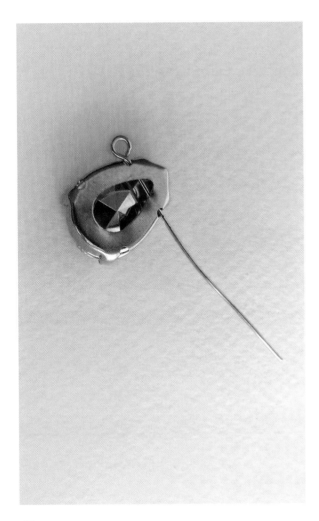

1 Slide an eye pin through the holes in the setting of one of the rhinestones.

2 Trimming the wire of the eye pin with wire cutters if necessary, bend the straight end of the pin into a loop the same size as the loop on the other end with the round nose pliers. Repeat with the other two rhinestones, adding the eye pins and bending the ends into loops.

❸ Open one jump ring by using two sets of pliers to grab on either side of the seam in the ring. Twist the pliers and ends of the jump ring away from each other in a north-south motion. Use the jump ring to connect one of the rhinestone loops to the end of one of the 8-inch pieces of chain, then close the ring by twisting the ends back toward each other so the ends of the ring are flush.

❹ Open another jump ring and use it to attach the other side of the rhinestone to one of the 1-inch pieces of chain.

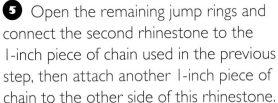

5 Open the remaining jump rings and connect the second rhinestone to the 1-inch piece of chain used in the previous step, then attach another 1-inch piece of chain to the other side of this rhinestone.

6 Use jump rings to attach the third rhinestone to the 1-inch piece of chain used in the previous step, then to attach the 8-inch piece of chain to the other side of the rhinestone.

7 To finish the necklace, add a jump ring to each end of the necklace, and attach a clasp on one of the rings before closing it.

LARIAT CHAIN *necklace*

Sometimes, a delicate chain necklace is all you need. Using simple thin chain, the lariat silhouette makes the statement for this necklace. It also layers well with other fine necklaces for a bolder look. In this variation of a lariat, the chain slides through a jump ring to adjust the length and doesn't need a clasp. Choose thin jump rings that fit through the links of your chain, and add a small charm or bead for a personal touch.

materials

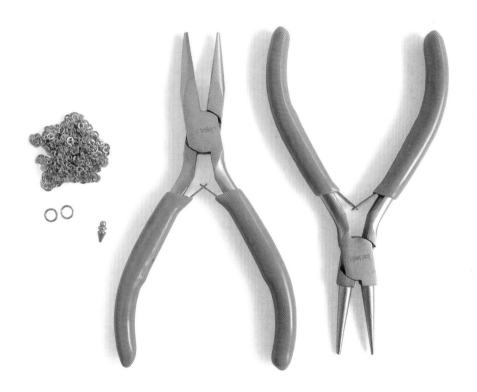

- 2 5mm jump rings
- Round-nose jewelry pliers
- Chain-nose jewelry pliers
- Small charm
- 26 inches of thin chain

❶ Open one jump ring by using two sets of pliers to grab on either side of the seam in the ring. Twist the pliers and ends of the jump rings away from each other in a north-south motion. Use the jump ring to connect the charm to one end of the chain, then close the ring by twisting the ends back toward each other so the ends of the ring are flush.

❷ Open up the second jump ring (as in Step 1) and hook it onto the other end of the chain. Before closing the jump ring, form an adjustable loop by looping the jump ring around the chain so the chain can slide through the ring while still connected at the other end.

3 To wear, just slide the necklace open by expanding the loop, pull over your head, and adjust.

This necklace is designed to adjust to wear. If you want a more fixed version, just attach a spring clasp to the second jump ring instead of looping the ring over the chain. To wear, clasp onto a link midway down the chain to make the Y shape of a lariat.

MIXED CHAIN
AND RIBBON
necklace

Once you begin crafting, you'll find yourself accumulating lots of leftover pieces from your projects. A few inches of leftover chain here, a strand of beads there, and soon you have a craft supply stash like most DIYers. Hanging on to those supplies and keeping old or broken jewelry is a resourceful way to make the most out of your materials, and it's fun to challenge yourself to use up the supplies you've been accruing. This necklace does exactly that—taking whatever chains you might have lying around and turning them into a chic necklace.

materials

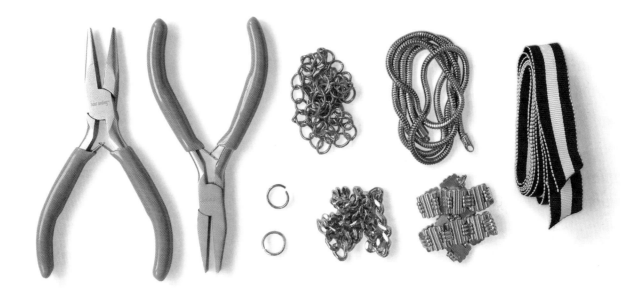

- 2 12mm jump rings
- Round-nose jewelry pliers
- Chain-nose jewelry pliers
- Mixed lengths of assorted chain
- 40 inches of ribbon, cut into two 20-inch pieces

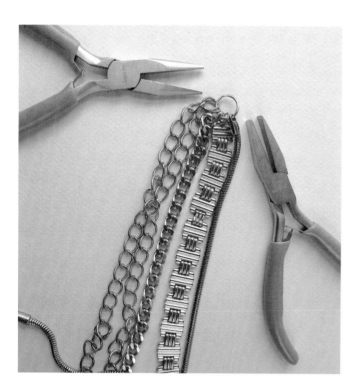

1 Open one of your jump rings by using two sets of pliers to grab on either side of the seam in the ring. Twist the pliers and ends of the jump rings away from each other in a north-south motion. Then slide the jump ring through the end links of your chains and close the ring by twisting the ends back toward each other so the ends of the ring are flush. You may want to double some of the chains. If this is the case, connect both ends of those chains to this first jump ring.

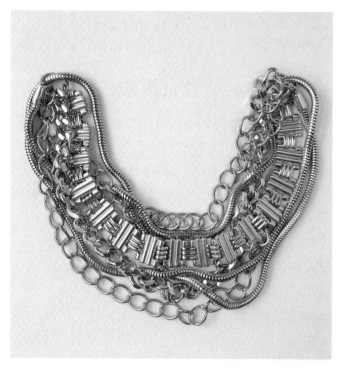

2 Open the second jump ring, attach it to the other ends of the chain, and close it. If doubling up some of the lengths of chain, connect the jump ring to the middle of the chain.

3 Tie the end of a ribbon to each of the jump rings.

4 Trim the ends of the ribbon. To wear, tie the ribbon in a bow.

STATEMENT NECKLACE SUPPLIES

For the different chains in this project, use up whatever you have on hand or look to vintage or cast-off jewelry to add interesting chains. Build up your own supply of old pieces by asking relatives for any baubles they no longer want, going to garage sales, or checking your local thrift store.

DELICATE LAYERED
necklace

While part of the fun of making and collecting jewelry is mixing, matching, and layering those pieces yourself, jewelry that takes the guesswork out of the equation is also fun and easy to wear. I've always loved the look of layered delicate necklaces, but sometimes the metals and lengths just don't work together. Solution? Make a simple DIY necklace that's already layered!

materials

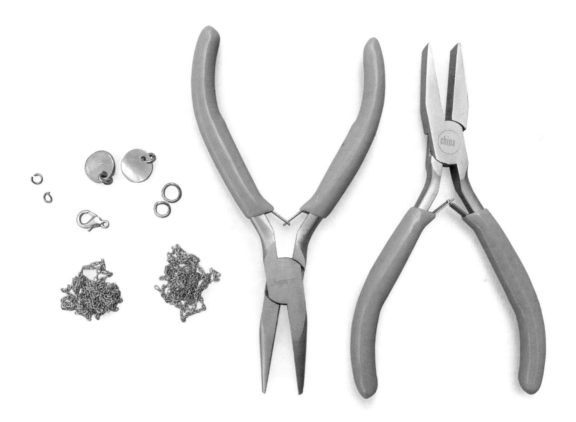

- 2 small (5mm) jump rings
- Round-nose jewelry pliers
- Flat-nose jewelry pliers
- 31 inches of delicate chain cut into one 15-inch piece and one 16-inch piece

- 2 medium (7mm) jump rings
- 2 charms
- Clasp

1 Open a small (5mm) jump ring by using two sets of pliers to grab on either side of the seam in the ring. Twist the pliers and ends of the jump ring away from each other in a north-south motion. Use the 5mm jump ring to connect the ends of the two pieces of chain to one of the 7mm jump rings, then close the jump ring by twisting the ends back toward each other so the ends of the ring are flush.

2 Slide the charms onto the chains.

❸ Open the other 7mm jump ring and close it around the clasp.

❹ Use the remaining 5mm jump ring to connect the loose ends of the chain to the 7mm ring attached to the clasp.

Chapter 3

CORD, STRING, AND RIBBON STATEMENTS

Beads and chain aren't the only materials for do-it-yourself jewelry! You've mastered the basics of jewelry-making and have an idea of what to do with various chains; the projects in this chapter borrow techniques and materials from other kinds of crafts, and teach you how to use cord, rope, ribbon, or even raffia in your customized jewelry. These supplies let you play with texture and color while adding unique handmade elements to your statement necklaces, plus there's a material to suit every mood, season, or style. Searching for a necklace that's sporty chic? Try a project with bungee cord or paracord, like the Knotted Bungee Necklace or Knotted Necklace, which are perfect for summer. Or, if you're in the mood for something more feminine, the Ruffled Ribbon Necklace uses sheer ribbon for a romantic feel that looks lovely on a lightweight sweater in spring or fall. When shopping for supplies, think outside the jewelry box by exploring the upholstery, knitting, sewing, and floral-arranging aisles of craft stores for your projects.

Also, while lengths for materials are listed for each project, an important tip when working with these unique supplies is to always have a little more than you think you'll need. Add a few extra inches of rope before cutting or buy an extra yard of ribbon to ensure you don't run out midway through your project.

Working with these different materials opens you up to a variety of techniques that you'll use in the projects in this chapter, as well as future DIYs, so get ready to wrap, tie, knot, ruffle, braid, and knit your way to one-of-a-kind handcrafted statement necklaces!

KNOTTED BUNGEE *necklace*

A looped and knotted necklace adds an easy nautical touch to your look. In this project, you'll master the art of the chain sinnet, a kind of knot used for shortening rope for use or storage. Bungee cord, available at large craft stores, gives the necklace a sporty feel, and makes the necklace's stretchy loop closure a breeze. Add a pop of neon from some brightly colored string, like mason twine, available at the hardware store.

materials

- 10 feet of bungee cord
- 4 feet of mason twine
- Scissors
- Fraying sealant, optional (see "Helpful Hints" sidebar in this project for more information)

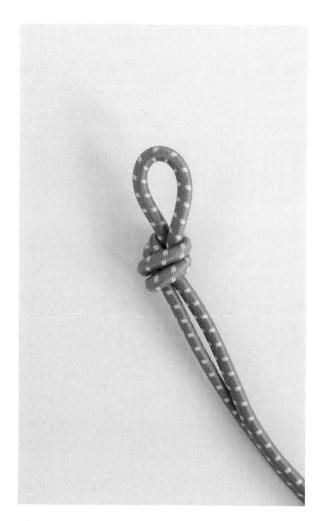

1 Bring together the ends of the bungee cord. At the folded end of the cord, tie the end around into a knot, leaving a small 1-inch loop.

2 Holding the loose ends of the cord together, measure 8 inches up from the loop. Then create a pretzel-shaped loop at that spot, keeping the knotted end on the left and the loose ends on the right.

3 Pinch the section of cords under the right loop of the pretzel, and pull up to create a new loop about 1½ inches long. While holding the new loop, gently tug on the knotted ends of the cord to tighten the cord around the new loop.

4 Reach through the new loop to pinch and pull the cord underneath, pulling on the side of the cord from the loose end, creating a second loop. Keep the loops a uniform size of about 1½ inches by gently pulling on the ends of the cord.

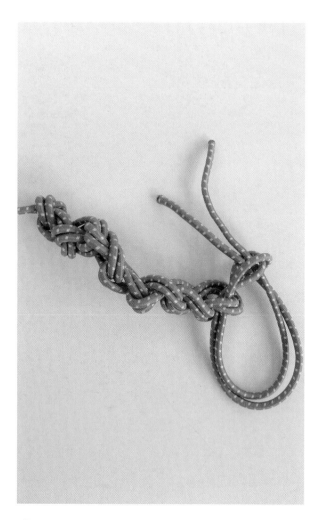

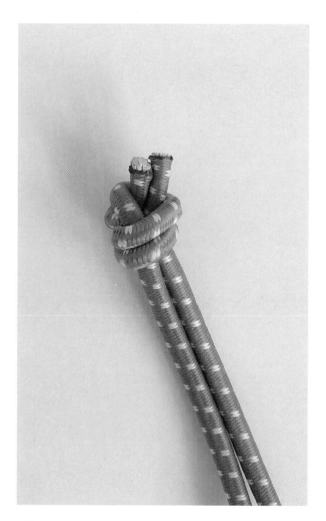

5 Repeat these steps until you have created a knotted section of about seven loops. When creating the final loop, pull the cord ends all the way through.

6 Tie the loose ends into an overhand knot. Line up both ends of the necklace to make sure they are even, then adjust the placement of the knot and trim the cord ends as needed.

7 Tie a long piece of bright string around the cord, next to the knotted portion, and wrap a section of the cords about 1 inch long with the string.

8 Tie off the string and trim the ends of the string. You can tuck the ends into the wrapped section to conceal them. Repeat on the other side of the necklace.

HELPFUL HINTS

Knots can be tricky to master, and practice makes perfect! Before beginning this project, practice tying a chain sinnet (they are easily undone). For extra help, watch the knot in action at *www.animatedknots.com/chainsinnet.*

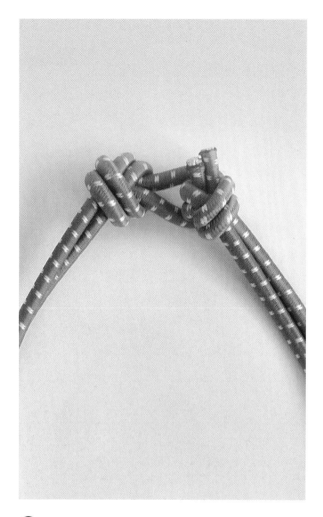

9 To clasp the necklace, push the knotted end through the 1-inch loop on the other side.

Prevent frayed cord ends with a dab of fraying sealant, found in the sewing section of craft stores. You can also use a drop of clear nail polish to seal ends together. For synthetic cords, such as those used in this project, gently fuse the ends by melting them slightly with a lighter. Keep the cord out of the flame, and watch out for your fingers. The melted cord will be hot, so be careful!

TASSEL *necklace*

nspired by vintage and modern pieces, this necklace is an easy DIY that has playful movement and texture. While this version has a monochromatic color scheme, you can play with the colors of your tassels or use silver or gold tassels for a metallic variation. Using premade tassels, the necklace is a snap to make. It's as easy as opening and closing a jump ring.

materials

- Scissors
- 5 2-inch tassels
- 8 7mm jump rings
- Round-nose jewelry pliers

- Chain-nose jewelry pliers
- 20 inches of 10mm curb chain
- Clasp

❶ Begin by using the scissors to trim the loop off of each tassel.

❷ Open one jump ring by using two sets of pliers to grab on either side of the seam in the ring. Twist the pliers and ends of the jump ring away from each other in a north-south motion. Once open, loop the jump ring through the top of the tassel. Repeat for all the tassels.

3 Beginning in the center of the chain, attach the tassels to the chain by looping the jump ring around a link and closing it by twisting the ends back toward each other so the ends of the ring are flush.

4 Continue to attach the tassels to the chain with the jump rings. Work from the center outward and space the tassels evenly ½ inch apart.

5 To finish the necklace, add a jump ring to each end of the necklace, and attach a clasp on one of the rings before closing it.

LEATHER CORD

With clean lines and a neutral palette, this minimalist necklace uses braided leather bolo cord, available online, which is offset by a thread-wrapped section. To cover up any loose ends and add a metallic detail, brass compression sleeves (from the plumbing section of the hardware store) make a great stand-in for beads.

materials

- Scissors
- 20 inches of 6mm cord, such as leather bolo cord
- 1 skein of embroidery thread
- Super glue
- 6 ¼-inch compression sleeves
- 2 6mm barrel cord ends
- 2 7mm jump rings
- Chain-nose jewelry pliers
- Round-nose jewelry pliers
- Clasp

① Cut the cord to your desired length of necklace, then measure the halfway point of the cord. Tie the embroidery thread to the cord about 2 inches to the left of the center point, where you will begin the wrapped section of the necklace. Start wrapping toward the center point of the cord, covering the loose end of the thread, creating a wrapped section about 4 inches long.

② Once the entire color-block section is wrapped, tie off and trim the end of the embroidery thread.

••● *Make It Yours!* ●••

Instead of neutral shades, you can also try wrapping multiple sections of the necklace in different colors, separating them with the compression sleeves for a bold variation.

3 Add a dab of glue to the knot in the embroidery thread and the cord.

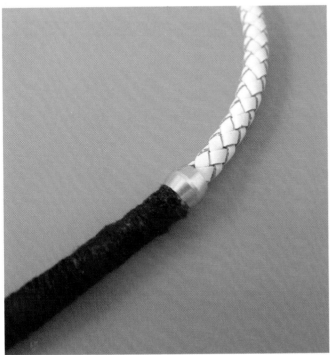

4 Slide a compression sleeve onto the cord and press firmly onto the glue, covering the knot in the thread. Add 2 additional compression sleeves to this end of the cord, then repeat to add the remaining three compression sleeves to the other side of the necklace.

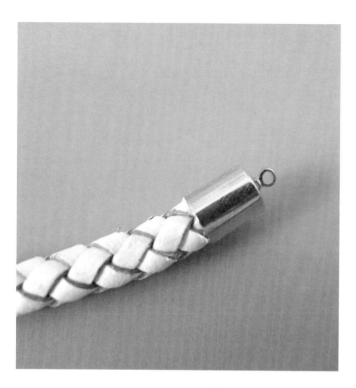

5 After adding a drop of glue into each cord end, slide the 6mm barrel cord ends onto each end of the cord and allow to dry according to glue directions.

6 Open your jump rings by using two sets of pliers to grab on either side of the seam in the ring. Twist the pliers and ends of the jump rings away from each other in a north-south motion. Attach the jump rings to each of the barrel cord ends, adding a clasp to one side. Then close each ring by twisting the ends back toward each other so the ends of the ring are flush.

FINGER KNIT
necklace

While projects made up of lots of materials and multiple steps can be very rewarding to accomplish, there is something satisfying about the simplicity of a DIY statement necklace that needs limited materials and uses just three of your fingers to make. Once you master the weaving and looping pattern of finger knitting, this necklace becomes incredibly relaxing to create, which makes this a great project to do while hanging out with friends or unwinding while watching a movie.

materials

- 6 yards of jersey t-shirt yarn, plus 2 1-yard pieces
- 2 copper tubes (called couplings, from the hardware store)
- Scissors

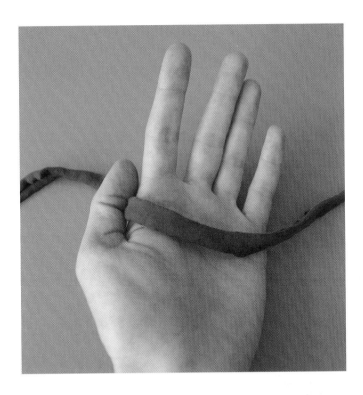

① To start, place a long 12-inch tail of yarn between your thumb and index finger, with the rest of the yarn lying across your palm.

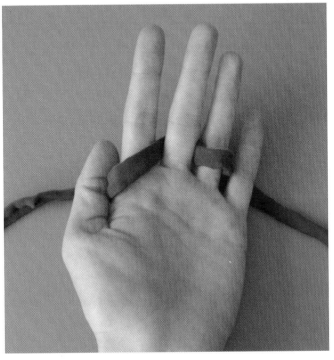

② Weave the yarn over your index finger, under your middle finger, over your ring finger, and under your pinky.

3 Wrap the end of the yarn over your pinky finger, then weave it back toward your thumb, going under your ring finger, over your middle finger, and under your index finger.

4 Repeat the weaving process twice more, working toward the pinky and back again to the thumb so that each finger has two loops on it. Lay the long end of the yarn across your palm.

5 Starting with the pinky, pull the bottom loop up and over the top loop. Let the pulled-up loop drop behind your finger.

6 Repeat for each finger so that each finger now only has one loop.

7 Take the long end of the yarn and weave it back over your fingers—over your index finger, under your middle finger, over your ring finger, and under your pinky. Then, weave the yarn back to your thumb—around and over your pinky, under your ring finger, and under your index finger.

8 Pull the bottom loops over the new loops as in the previous steps. Repeat the process of weaving toward the pinky and back to the thumb, then pulling the loops up and over. As you do so, a knit tail will take form on the back side of your hand. Gently tug the end each time you pull the loops over and off your fingers to pull the knit portion together.

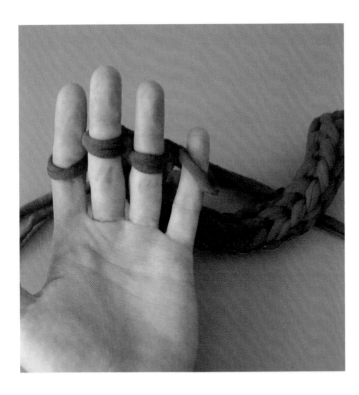

9 To "cast off" your finger knitting, leave a single row of loops on your fingers.

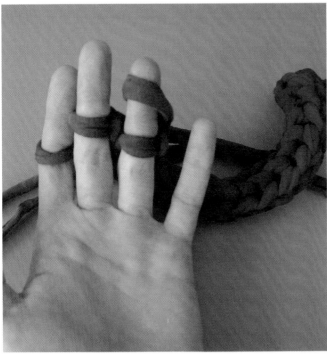

10 Lift the loop off of your pinky and onto your ring finger.

11 Lift the bottom loop of the ring finger up and over the top loop and off of the finger.

12 Do the same for the loop on the ring finger, moving it over to the middle finger, then repeat for the middle finger's loop onto the index finger.

13 Pull the bottom loop on the index finger over and off. Pull the end of the yarn through the last loop, and pull tight.

14 Take one of the 1-yard reserved pieces of yarn and thread it halfway through some of the loops at the end of the knit section.

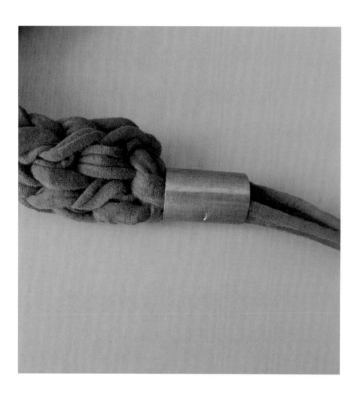

15 Slide a copper tube onto the three strands of yarn and knot the yarn in place above the tube.

16 Repeat with the second 1-yard yarn piece and copper tube at the other end of the necklace.

17 Try on the necklace by tying behind your neck, making note of how much excess yarn remains. Untie, then trim the ends of the yarn so that they are even.

STATEMENT NECKLACE SUPPLIES

Jersey yarn, which is available in solid colors or patterns, is made of the same stretchy material as your favorite comfy tee, and is also known as t-shirt yarn. Some yarn manufacturers even use upcycled fabric off-cuts, the unused pieces from the end of the roll of cloth. Instead of ending up in the landfill, in your hands these scraps can become a unique necklace!

RUFFLED
RIBBON
necklace

A pretty ruffled ribbon necklace is an easy way to add a feminine touch to an otherwise basic neckline, jazzing up even the most basic tee. This project bridges different crafts by bringing sewing supplies and techniques to your jewelry-making. However, the only hand-sewing skill you need to know is the easy running stitch: a straight stitch created by simply passing the needle in and out of the fabric. For a fun twist, try strips of fabric scraps instead of ribbon.

materials

- Needle and 4 feet of beading string or thread
- 14 inches of thin chain, cut into two 7-inch pieces
- 1 yard of 1-inch ribbon
- 60–70 small faceted beads

- Scissors
- 2 7mm jump rings
- Round-nose jewelry pliers
- Chain-nose jewelry pliers
- Clasp

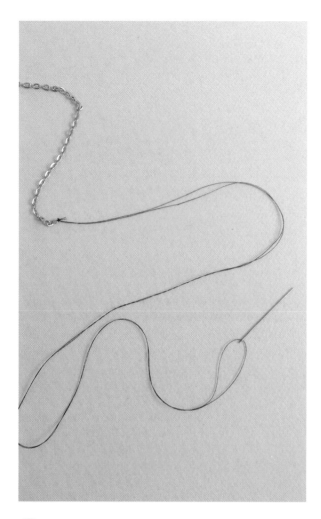

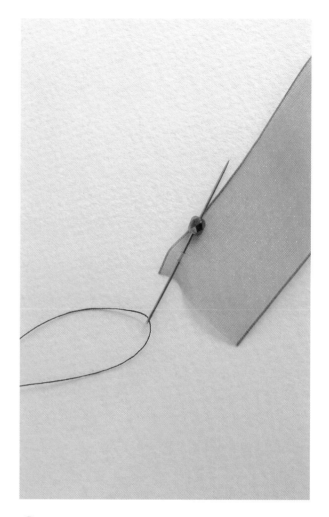

❶ Thread the needle with the long, 4-foot piece of thread, double it up, and knot the ends onto the end of one of the 7-inch pieces of chain.

❷ Push the needle through the ribbon (about ⅛ an inch from the ribbon's edge) and out again, then add a bead to the needle before pushing the needle back through to the underside of the ribbon.

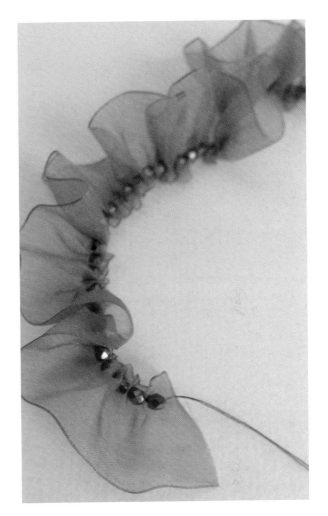

3 Continue making running stitches about ⅛ inch apart, gathering the ribbon as you go to create ruffles and adding beads in between the folds. For extra dimension and variety, occasionally sew two folds in the ribbon before adding the bead.

4 Repeat until you've reached your desired length or come to the end of the ribbon. Securely tie the thread to the end of the second 7-inch piece of chain and trim loose ends.

5 Finally, open your jump rings by using two sets of pliers to grab on either side of the seam in the ring. Twist the pliers and ends of the jump rings away from each other in a north-south motion. Attach a jump ring to each end of the necklace, add a clasp to one side, then close each ring by twisting the ends back toward each other so the ends of the ring are flush.

STATEMENT NECKLACE SUPPLIES

When choosing a ribbon for this project, select a lightweight material that will be easy to sew through and fold into ruffles. Woven ribbons, such as gossamer, organdy, and even grosgrain, work better than ribbons made of stiffer materials like velvet, satin, or jacquard ribbon.

RAFFIA
necklace

Evocative of straw beach bags and sun hats, raffia is quintessentially a warm-weather material, which makes it ideal for a spring or summer necklace that celebrates the season. You can buy easy-to-work-with raffia ribbon in spools of many colors for only a few dollars and have plenty left over for other projects. While tying the strands of raffia around the rhinestone chain is the most time-consuming part of the project, this necklace should still only take you about 45 minutes or less to complete.

materials

- Spool of ¼-inch raffia ribbon, cut in 27 6-inch pieces
- Scissors
- 6 inches of 6mm rhinestone chain
- 2 fold-over cord ends or 6mm rhinestone cup chain connectors
- Round-nose jewelry pliers
- Chain-nose jewelry pliers
- Super glue
- 4 7mm jump rings
- 14 inches of chain, cut into two 7-inch pieces
- Clasp

❶ Fold a 6-inch piece of raffia in half, forming a loop. Lay the folded raffia over the rhinestone chain, in the space between individual rhinestones, with the loop 1 inch above the chain. Pull the loop behind and around the chain, then feed the two ends of the raffia through the loop. Pull the ends to tighten the loop up to the chain. Repeat to add a piece of raffia to each of the spaces between the rhinestones.

❷ To fill out the necklace, loop the raffia pieces around the rhinestones. To do this, fold a piece of raffia in half, forming a loop, and lay the folded raffia over the rhinestone, so that the rhinestone is in between either side of the raffia loop. Pull the loop behind and around the rhinestone, sliding the ends of the raffia through the loop and pulling to tighten the knot up to the rhinestone. Leave the end rhinestones without raffia.

❸ If using fold-over cord ends, open them up with pliers and add a drop of glue to each. Then press them onto the back of the last rhinestones and let dry according to glue directions.

❹ If using rhinestone cup chain connectors, add a small dab of glue to the cup and place the rhinestone setting inside. Use your pliers to gently fold over the prongs of the cup to secure and allow the glue to dry according to its directions.

5 Open the jump rings by using two sets of pliers to grab on either side of the seam in the ring. Twist the pliers and ends of the jump rings away from each other in a north-south motion. Attach the jump rings to the fold-over ends or cup chain connectors and to one end of each of the chains. Then close the ring by twisting the ends back toward each other so the ends of the ring are flush.

6 Finally, open and attach a jump ring to each end of the necklace, add a clasp to one side, then close the rings.

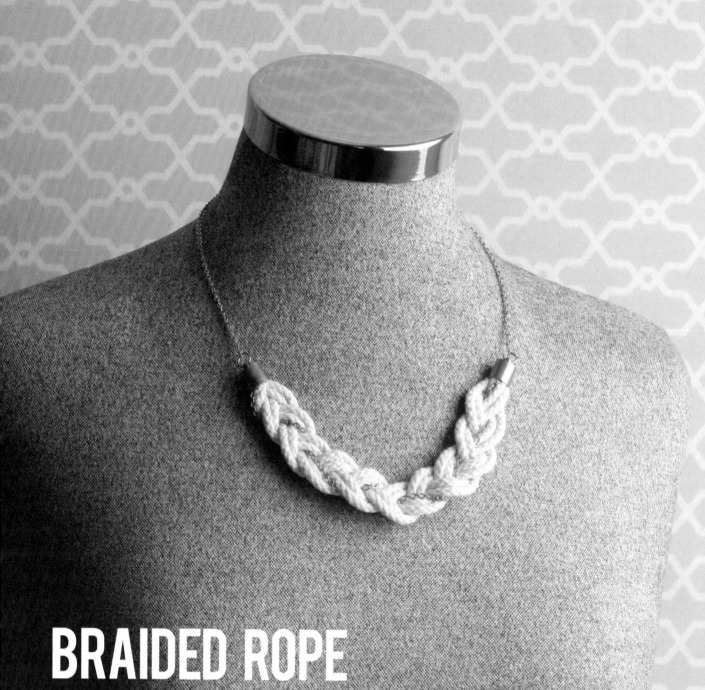

BRAIDED ROPE
AND CHAIN
necklace

ome of the best DIY projects come from using unusual materials from unexpected places. This necklace features braided clothesline that you can buy at the hardware store with thin chain woven throughout for extra shine. Bright cord like paracord would work just as well for a colorful variation in place of the clothesline. Often with DIY jewelry-making, messy ends can make a piece look unfinished, so make sure your projects look polished by using cord ends like the ones at the end of the braid in this necklace.

materials

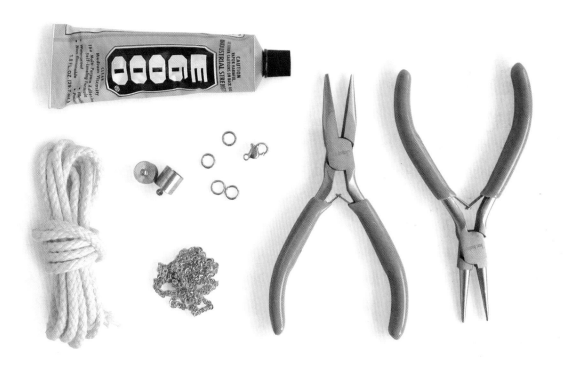

- 6 feet of ¼-inch thick rope, cut into three 2-foot pieces
- 6 inches of masking tape
- 17 inches of thin chain, cut into two 7-inch pieces and one 10-inch piece

- Scissors
- Super glue
- 2 10mm barrel cord ends
- 4 7mm jump rings
- Round-nose jewelry pliers

- Chain-nose jewelry pliers
- Clasp

❶ Fold the lengths of rope in half. Tape them at the folded ends along with the 10-inch piece of chain. Keeping the chain with one of the ropes, and treating each folded rope as one strand, braid the rope pieces together.

❷ Braid to the end of the ropes and chain, then tape the ends together. Trim the taped end to ½ inch by using the scissors to cut through the tape and rope. Measure ½ inch up the tape, then use the scissors to trim the rope through the tape.

3 Add a small dab of glue to the inside of one of the barrel cord ends and push the cord end over the taped ends of the braid. Repeat on the other end of the braid and let dry according to glue directions.

4 Use the jump rings to connect the smaller pieces of chain to each cord end. Open two jump rings by using two sets of pliers to grab on either side of the seam in the ring. Twist the pliers and ends of the jump rings away from each other in a north-south motion. Attach the jump rings to the cord ends and to one end of each of the chains. Then close each ring by twisting the ends back toward each other so the ends of the ring are flush.

5 Finally, open and attach a jump ring to each end of the necklace, add a clasp to one side, then close the rings.

STATEMENT NECKLACE SUPPLIES

Barrel cord ends are sometimes difficult to track down in stores, but are easy to find online. A quick search will yield websites selling the cord ends, which range in size and are perfect for finishing all sorts of cord jewelry projects.

KNOTTED
necklace

In this necklace, a decorative knot becomes the focal point for brightly colored cord. The knot used in this project is relatively simple, but tutorials are available online, on websites like *www .fusionknots.com*, for other styles, such as Celtic knots or heart-shaped knots. The jump rings on each side of the knot are optional, but they make the necklace look polished and keep the cords together for a cleaner look. Two colors of cord are used in this tutorial to demonstrate the knot-tying techniques, but you can try any combination of cords and colors!

materials

- 52 inches of paracord, cut into two 26-inch pieces
- 2 12mm jump rings
- Round-nose jewelry pliers
- Chain-nose jewelry pliers
- Scissors
- 2 7mm jump rings
- Clasp
- 2 12mm barrel cord ends
- Super glue

1 Fold each piece of paracord in half, then bend halfway into a loop about 2 inches big.

2 Lay one of the paracord loops down horizontally so the round end of the loop faces toward the left, with the top end of the paracord crossing over the bottom end. Lay the other piece of paracord horizontally on top of the first piece, but make sure the loop is facing toward the right, with the top end of the paracord crossing over the bottom end, forming a 2-inch loop. The loops should overlap the crossed section of the cord.

3 Weave the top end of the right-facing loop under the top of the left-facing loop and back over the bottom end of the right-facing loop. Uncross the top end of the left-facing loop to weave under its bottom end and over the bottom end of the right-facing loop.

4 Weave the top end of the right-facing loop through and under the bottom of the left-facing loop.

5 Pull the ends of both lengths of paracord to tighten the knot. Adjust the cords so they lie flat in the knot, then gather the loose ends on each side of the knot together at the top corners of the knot.

6 Open a 12mm jump ring by using two sets of pliers to grab on either side of the seam in the ring. Twist the pliers and ends of the jump ring away from each other in a north-south motion. Hook the jump ring around the cords, close to the knot, to keep the cords in place. Then close the ring by twisting the ends back toward each other so the ends of the ring are flush. Repeat on the other side.

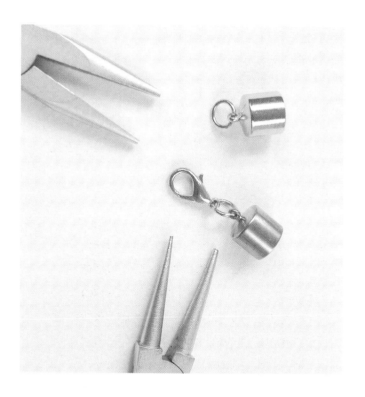

7 Attach the 7mm jump rings and clasp to the 2 barrel cord ends.

HELPFUL HINTS

This project is a quick one! Glue drying time aside, this project should only take you about 20 minutes after you learn the knot.

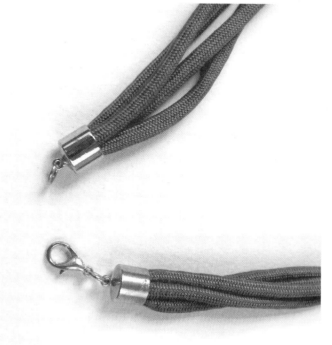

8 Trim the ends of the cord even. Add a drop of glue to the inside of the barrel cord ends and slide onto the ends of the paracord. Allow the glue to dry according to package instructions.

Chapter 4

DESIGNER-INSPIRED STATEMENTS

Ever fall in love with a gorgeous necklace you saw in a magazine or online but balk at the price tag? In these situations, it's the perfect time to DIY instead of buy! From runway to retailers, designer jewelry offers a huge range of inspiration for your next DIY project. This is ideal for those times when you're itching to create but aren't sure where to start, or when you want to put your own spin on a trend or design. The projects in this chapter were inspired by works of today's noteworthy jewelry designers, such as Mawi, Lizzie Fortunato, and Fallon; their necklaces stimulate ideas for materials, techniques, and styles.

For special pieces like these, it's sometimes worth spending a little extra money on higher-quality materials to keep the necklaces looking as luxe as their original counterparts. So feel free to splurge on real gold or silver jewelry findings instead of cheaper base metals like brass, or on Swarovski crystals instead of plastic rhinestones. Even with these little indulgences, you're bound to save as you get the look for less. Let these designer-inspired pieces dress up your favorite t-shirts and jeans, or match them with a favorite dress and a great pair of earrings for an easy, party-ready look.

JEWELED FRINGE
necklace

Mix fancy with fun in this playful necklace inspired by the fringed styles of jewelry designer Joomi Lim, who is known for her eclectic combinations of textures, such as fringe with rhinestones or tough spikes with ladylike pearls. This project is the perfect modern update for a vintage rhinestone necklace and, since the necklace is sewn to the fringe, it doesn't cause any permanent alteration to the vintage piece. If you're unable to find a vintage necklace, look for affordable rhinestone necklaces at stores and add your own flair with the fringe!

materials

- 5 inches of 2-inch fringe trim
- 5 inches of 4-inch fringe trim
- 14–18 inch rhinestone necklace

- Needle and 4 feet of thread in color matching the fringe
- Scissors

① Layer the 2-inch fringe trim on top of the 4-inch fringe, then center the necklace on top of the fringe.

② Hand-sew the fringe to the necklace, using a whip stitch. To do a whipstitch, make small, angled stitches that go between the rhinestones and over the top of the trim to behind the back of the necklace. Bring the needle back up from behind the necklace below the space between the next set of rhinestones. Sew a stitch between each of the rhinestones and around the connecting chain of the necklace.

3 Once you've reached the end of the trim, securely knot and trim the thread to finish the necklace.

HELPFUL HINTS

If you want to add more length to the necklace, use jump rings to attach a few inches of chain and a clasp to the ends of the necklace.

BRAIDED JEWEL *necklace*

While jewelry designers are a great source of DIY ideas, even your favorite stores online or at the mall can inspire your next project! This project was based on a necklace found a few seasons ago at a retail store. In a rich and quintessentially fall color that is ready to top off your favorite sweater, the square knot macramé construction is simple to do and easy to embellish your own way with sew-on rhinestones.

materials

- 6 yards of silk rattail cord, cut into 1 3-foot piece and 1 15-foot piece
- 2 inches of curb chain
- Large clasp
- Scissors

- Fabric glue
- 9 sew-on rhinestones in settings
- Needle and 6 feet of thread in the same color as the cord

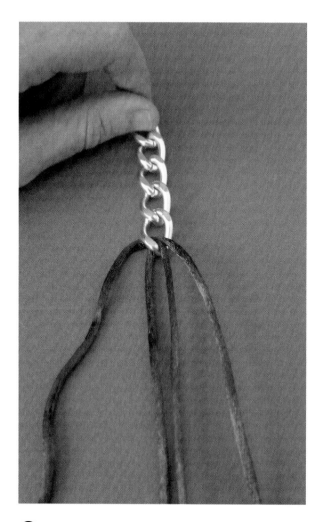
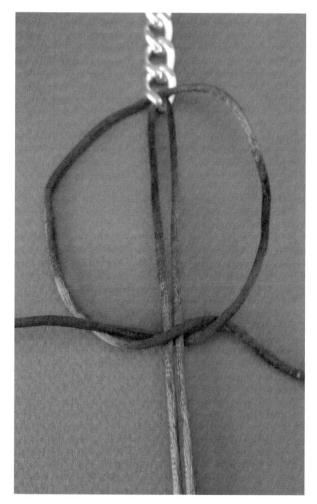

❶ Thread both lengths of cord evenly through the last link of the chain, with the shorter cord inside the longer.

❷ Tie a square knot with the strands of the outer cord around the shorter inner cord. First, take the longer string on the left and cross it over the shorter middle strands, making a loop that looks like the number 4. Then cross the right long strand over the loose end of the first strand.

3 Next, pull the right strand under the center strings and the loop of the left string. Then, pull both the right and left ends tight to make the knot.

4 Repeat on the opposite side, by making a loop with the right string and bringing the left string under the center strings and through the loop. Pull tight and continue forming knots, alternating sides, for the entire length of the necklace.

5 Once you've reached the desired length of the necklace, tightly tie the cord to the clasp and trim the ends. Add a few dabs of fabric glue to hold the knot and prevent the ends of the cord from unraveling.

6 To attach the rhinestones, add a small drop of fabric glue to the back of the rhinestone and press in place on the necklace. Repeat as needed. After the glue has dried, hand-sew the jewels in place to further secure, passing the needle and thread through the holes on the edges of the rhinestones.

SEQUIN
TRIM
necklace

This statement necklace is inspired by the intricate beadwork of the necklaces from textile designer turned jewelry artist Fiona Paxton, but this DIY necklace takes a significant shortcut. Instead of hand-embroidering the beadwork, this project substitutes geometric-patterned sequin trim topped with layers of draped chain to make a standout piece. Similar styles have been spotted on celebrities such as Kate Moss and Rihanna, so embrace their rocker-meets-globetrotter look by pairing this necklace with slouchy boots or a moto jacket.

materials

- Fabric glue
- 26 inches of sequined trim
- 10 5mm jump rings
- Round-nose jewelry pliers
- Flat-nose jewelry pliers
- 70 inches of chain, cut into five pieces that are 13, 13½, 14, 14½, and 15 inches long

① Begin by adding glue to the end of the trim on the wrong (back) side. Fold the end of the trim over about 1 inch and press in place to stick. Repeat on the other end of the trim and let dry according to package instructions.

② Open a jump ring by using two sets of pliers to grab on either side of the seam in the ring. Twist the pliers and ends of the jump ring away from each other in a north-south motion. Push the open jump ring through the corner fabric of one of the folded ends of the trim, along the trim's inner edge. Attach the shortest (13-inch) piece of chain and close the ring by twisting the ends back toward each other so the ends of the ring are flush.

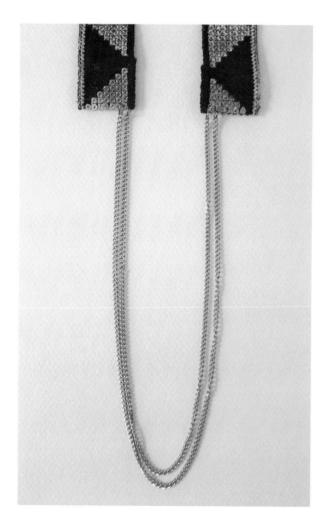

❸ Attach the other end of the chain to the other end of the trim in the same way, making sure to connect the jump ring to the fabric on the inner end of the trim.

❹ Repeat to attach the next-shortest (13½-inch) chain with jump rings on the outside of the first chain on each end of the sequin trim, approximately ³⁄₁₆ inch apart.

5 Working from the inside out, add the remaining pieces of chain from shortest to longest, spacing them evenly.

SPIKED CHAIN
necklace

British jewelry design company Mawi has mastered statement pieces that are both luxurious and edgy, like their chain, crystal, and spike necklace. Rather than spending a few hundred dollars on one of their designs, re-create the look for a whole lot less money and a little effort. Pick up bags of spike charms and jump rings in bulk so you have enough to complete the project. A word to the wise—opening and closing the large number of jump rings can be time-consuming, so work on this necklace in pieces at a time or while relaxing in front of the TV!

materials

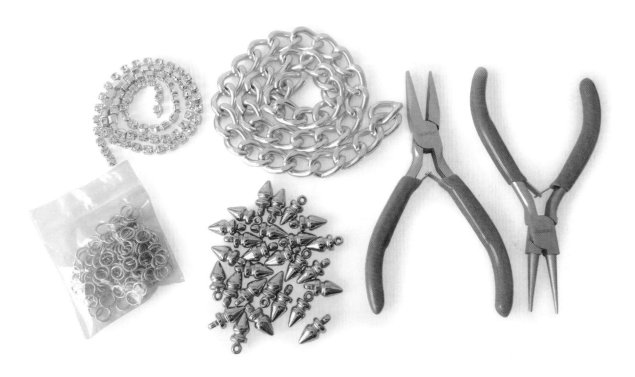

- 18 inches of 4mm rhinestone chain
- 18 inches of 12mm curb chain
- 40 7mm jump rings
- Round-nose jewelry pliers

- Chain-nose jewelry pliers
- 17 spike charms
- Clasp

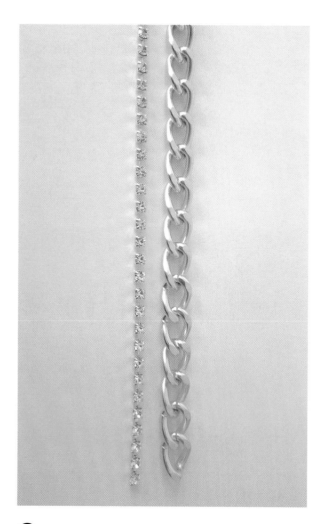

1 Line up the rhinestone chain and the curb chain, then measure the chains to locate the center link of both chains.

2 Open a jump ring by using two sets of pliers to grab onto either side of the seam in the ring. Twist the pliers and ends of the jump rings away from each other in a north-south motion. Loop the jump ring onto the center link of the curb chain and add a spike charm.

3 Next, hook the jump ring around the middle of the rhinestone chain and close each ring by twisting the ends back toward each other so the ends of the ring are flush.

4 Repeat to add more spikes on either side of the center, spacing the rings and charms evenly (every two rhinestones) on both chains and creating a spiked section roughly 10 inches long.

5 Once all the spikes have been added, use the jump rings to continue to evenly connect the two chains on either side of the spiked section of the necklace.

6 Finally, open and attach a jump ring to each end of the necklace, add a clasp to one side, then close the rings.

CRYSTAL SPIKE *necklace*

In the mood for a major-impact necklace? Look no further than this project, a glam and edgy necklace inspired by Fallon's classic designs. While there are several steps involved in making this necklace, the technique of pushing head pins through the sew-on settings of crystals and gluing the crystals and spikes together is straightforward. It's important to note that this necklace should be made in two stages. After you glue together the crystals and spikes to make the pendants, you'll need to let them sit overnight so the glue can fully cure. Once dry, you can begin attaching them to the chain.

materials

- 7 head pins
- 16 sew-on crystals in settings (3 12mm round, 7 7mm round, and 6 15mm marquis)
- Super glue

- 6 ½-inch cone spikes, with the screw attachments removed
- Round-nose jewelry pliers
- Wire cutters
- Chain-nose jewelry pliers

- 16 inches of curb chain
- 2 7mm jump rings
- Clasp

① Start by laying out the design of the necklace and deciding where you will place the crystals. The following instructions are for making the necklace design shown in the photos, but you can create your own design using different sizes and shapes of crystals.

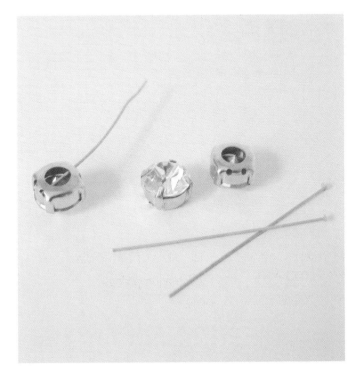

② To create the center focal point of the necklace, first push a head pin through the holes of one of the larger round crystals.

❸ Next, put a dab of glue on a marquis crystal and attach this to the large crystal by pressing into place. Repeat to add additional crystals to the focal point and allow to dry per package instructions.

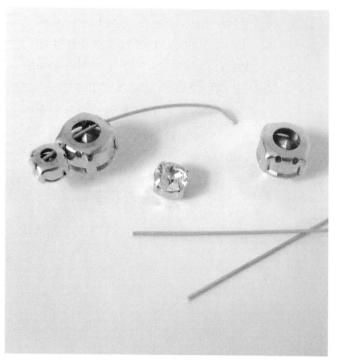

❹ To create the small pendants, start by pushing a head pin through a small round crystal and then through a large round crystal.

5 Next, add a drop of glue to a spike and press firmly onto the bottom, smaller crystal. Repeat to create a second small pendant and let dry.

STATEMENT NECKLACE SUPPLIES

Spending more on crystal rhinestones, instead of plastic or glass, is worth the investment. You can purchase online from bead stores or suppliers like Swarovski. The result is a more high-end appearance that will have everyone begging to know where you bought your necklace!

6 Use the same process to make the last four pendant pieces for the necklace, but this time push the head pins through only the marquis crystals. Then, glue the marquis crystals to the small 7mm crystals and spikes. When making the crystal pendants, remember that the design should mirror itself on either side of the focal point.

7 Once all the crystal pendants have dried overnight, use the round-nose pliers to bend the head pin wire at a 90-degree angle, then use the wire cutters to trim the head pins to about ½ inch.

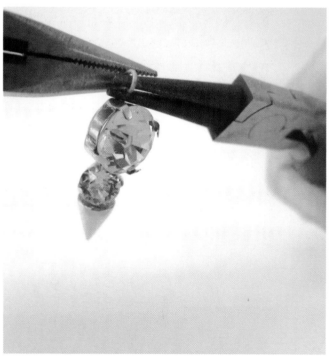

8 Hold the wire below the bend with the round–nose pliers. Then, grip the end of the wire with the round-nose pliers and bend the wire around the round pliers to form a loop. Be sure to leave the loop open.

9 Hook the loop of the focal pendant around the center link of the chain and bend the loop shut. Attach the rest of the pendants to the chain, spacing them evenly, about 1 inch apart.

10 Open your jump rings by using two sets of pliers to grab on either side of the seam in the ring. Twist the pliers and ends of the jump rings away from each other in a north-south motion. Attach a jump ring to each end of the necklace, add a clasp to one side, then close each ring by twisting the ends back toward each other so the ends of the ring are flush.

TURQUOISE TRIANGLE
necklace

Some designers just master the art of earthy and luxe. The sister duo behind jewelry company Lizzie Fortunato have the art down to a science and, season after season, they share necklaces that combine the natural look of stones with touches of glam gold and cord. Fortunately, you can master the look yourself in this easy DIY. Don't be intimidated by the laundry list of materials; the key is to choose a few beads you love and top them off with the polished look of cord and cord ends to achieve the blend of styles.

materials

- 18 inches of beading wire
- 1 small binder clip
- 13 turquoise triangle beads
- 5 8mm gold disc beads
- 8 10mm black disc beads
- 2 crimp beads

- 2 wire guards (optional)
- 4 6mm barrel cord ends
- Chain-nose jewelry pliers
- Flat-nose jewelry pliers
- Wire cutters
- Super glue

- 14 inches of beading cord, cut into two 7-inch pieces
- 2 7mm jump rings
- Clasp

❶ Secure one end of the beading wire with a small binder clip, then string all of the beads onto the beading wire in your choice of pattern.

HELPFUL HINTS

While you can purchase special beading guards to prevent your beads from sliding off the stringing material, a small binder clip on the wire can keep your designs in place!

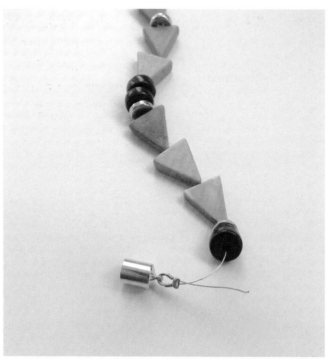

❷ On the loose end of the wire, slide a crimp bead and feed the beading wire through the wire guard, if using. Hook the beading wire around the loop of a barrel cord end, then feed the wire back through the crimp bead. Pull the wire tight and press the crimp closed with the pliers.

3 Trim the loose ends of the wire or tuck inside the beads. Repeat on the other end of the beads.

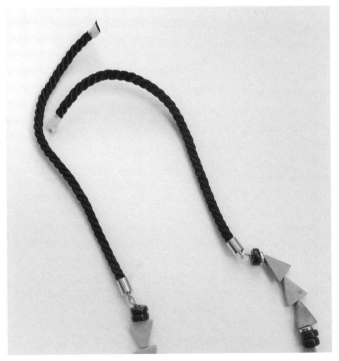

4 Put a small drop of glue inside each of the four cord ends and press them onto the ends of the two pieces of beading cord. Then wait for the glue to dry according to package instructions.

5 Once the glue dries, open your jump rings by using two sets of pliers to grab on either side of the seam in the ring. Twist the pliers and ends of the jump rings away from each other in a north-south motion. Attach a jump ring to each end of the necklace, add a clasp to one side, then close each ring by twisting the ends back toward each other so the ends of the ring are flush.

STATEMENT NECKLACE SUPPLIES

Wire guards, little horseshoe-shaped tubes, protect your beading wire from wear. While optional, they're great for keeping the beading wire from slipping through the ends of a jump ring. When using, simply slide the wire through the guard, and hook around the component you're connecting to the wire.

Chapter 5

SPECIAL OCCASION STATEMENTS

Whether dressing for a party, special event, or night out, no outfit is complete without a statement necklace to add personality to your look. Making your own necklace is a guaranteed way to ensure that your jewelry coordinates and complements your ensemble, so you'll always have something to wear! As with other projects in this book, measurements are given for the supplies, but you should feel free to tweak those measurements to lengthen or shorten a necklace so it works with the neckline of your dress or top. With these special occasion statement pieces, don't worry about being subtle. Instead, roll out the sparkle and metallics! Play with materials such as crystals and sequins in a bold way. And breathe new life into antique pieces by repurposing vintage materials for projects such as the Vintage Chandelier Pendant Necklace and the Rhinestone Pendants Necklace. Whichever necklaces you choose to make from this chapter, get ready to flaunt a beautiful handmade creation at any and every event your social calendar holds!

PEARL AND CRYSTAL
necklace

Pearls are an easy go-to for any formal occasion, but this DIY gives them a special twist by using extra large, faux-pearl beads and gold chain for a modern take. Add a touch of sparkle with crystal rondelle spacer beads, often used in beaded charm bracelets. Far from basic, this necklace livens up any little black dress and transitions easily from desk to drinks.

materials

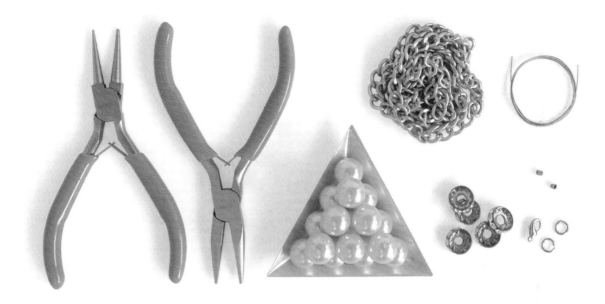

- 18 inches of beading wire
- 30 inches of chain, cut into one 19-inch piece and two 5½-inch pieces
- 2 crimp beads
- Round-nose jewelry pliers
- Chain-nose jewelry pliers

- 16 large faux-pearl beads
- 5 12mm crystal rondelle spacer beads
- 2 7mm jump rings
- Clasp

① Loop the end of the beading wire around the end link of one of the shorter pieces of chain, then slide a crimp bead onto the wire and fold the wire down and back through the crimp bead, forming a loop. Slide the crimp bead toward the chain to tighten and, using the pliers, flatten the crimp bead by pressing tightly.

② Next, decide on the pattern for your pearls and crystal rondelle beads. String the beads onto the wire.

••● Make It Yours! ●••

This necklace is a great project for experimenting with lengths and adding additional layers of chain. Try out different lengths to find what suits you best, add another length of chain for extra dimension, or opt out of the additional layers of chain altogether for a simple look!

3 Slide the other crimp bead onto the wire. Loop the wire around the end of the second short piece of chain and back through the crimp bead, pulling tight and securing with a crimp bead. Trim the excess wire.

4 Lay out the necklace and the 19-inch chain together in an oval shape, with the chain on the inside. Attach the two pieces at each end using the jump rings. Open the jump rings by using two sets of pliers to grab on either side of the seam in the ring. Twist the pliers and ends of the jump rings away from each other in a north-south motion. Attach a jump ring to each end of the combined necklace and chain. Add a clasp to one side, then close each ring by twisting the ends back toward each other so the ends of the ring are flush.

VINTAGE
CHANDELIER PENDANT
necklace

ome of the best DIY projects come from repurposed materials, like this pendant necklace made from a vintage chandelier crystal, which can be found at an antique or thrift store. Because the crystal is designed to catch the light, it's sure to sparkle with whatever you wear! The wire that comes on chandelier crystals is usually stronger than jewelry wire, so use heavy-duty tools when removing the original wire to keep your jewelry tools in good shape.

materials

- Wire cutters
- Chandelier crystal
- 18 inches of 24-gauge beading wire

- Chain-nose pliers
- 28 inches of chain

1 Clip off any original wire from the crystal.

2 Slide the beading wire a few inches through the hole in the crystal and bend up both ends of the wire, forming a checkmark shape.

3 With the pliers, twist the short end and the long end of the wire together, staying close to the crystal.

4 Bend the short end of the wire into a loop and wrap the extra wire below the loop around the first twist.

5 Begin wrapping the long end of the wire around the twists, then wrap it down and around the crystal.

6 Once the wrapped section reaches the drilled hole in the crystal, clip the wire and bend into a right angle.

7 Tuck the bent end of the wire into the hole of the crystal. Then, using the pliers, open up one of the end links on the chain. Loop the pendant and the link on the other end of the chain through the open loop, then close with the pliers to make a continuous chain.

STUDDED ZIPPER *lariat*

Pyramid studs are a DIYer's dream and they've come a long way since upholstery and leather jackets. However, folding over all those little prongs on studs can be a chore, which is why a studded trim like the one used in this project is a lifesaver. Here, all you have to do is cut a row of studs off the trim, which is available online or in the trim section of fabric stores, and attach it to a long zipper to create an easy but edgy necklace. This unique necklace is perfect for nights out when you want to toughen up your look!

materials

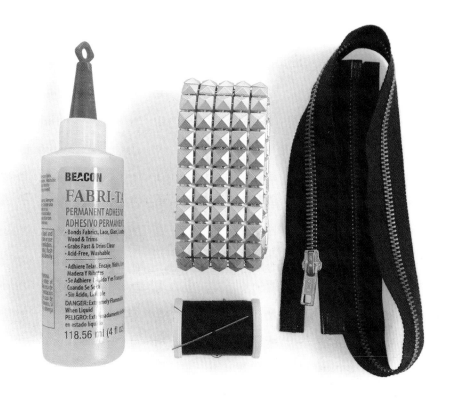

- 1 20-inch zipper
- Needle and 2 feet of thread in the same color as the zipper fabric
- ½ yard studded trim

- Scissors
- Fabric glue

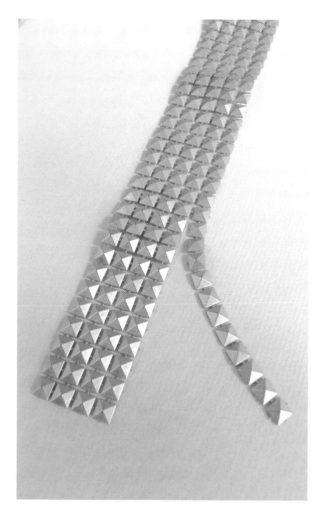

① Unzip the zipper and put the two top ends together, one on top of the other and overlapping a bit. Hand-sew into place with a few quick stitches

② Cut two rows of studs off the trim, each 20 inches long.

③ Glue the trim along both sides of the zipper and let dry according to package instructions.

STATEMENT NECKLACE SUPPLIES

What to do with extra trim? Try making a cuff bracelet with the trim attached to a piece of leather that wraps around your wrist, or embellish an old clutch or purse for an easy update.

RHINESTONE PENDANTS
necklace

Brooches, belt buckles, shoe clips, and dress clips (popular in the 1920s through 1940s for embellishing the necklines of dresses) now can be found in antique stores or online in many gorgeous styles. Breathe new life into this old rhinestone costume jewelry by repurposing it into a gorgeous Rhinestone Pendants Necklace. Can't find any vintage costume jewelry that suits your fancy? Modern versions of similar rhinestone pieces, such as buckles, are also available online or in trim supply stores. Attaching them to a simple chain creates a one-of-a-kind piece ready for any evening when you need a little elegance.

materials

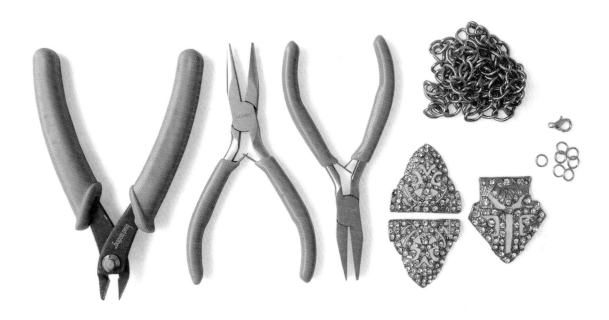

- Wire cutters
- 3 vintage rhinestone clips or buckles
- 8 10mm jump rings
- Chain-nose jewelry pliers

- Flat-nose jewelry pliers
- 18 inches of chain
- Clasp

1 Use the wire cutters to break off the clip or buckle hardware on the rhinestone pieces.

2 Open your jump rings by using two sets of pliers to grab on either side of the seam in the ring. Twist the pliers and ends of the jump rings away from each other in a north-south motion. Use the jump rings to attach the rhinestone piece to the middle of the chain, then close each ring by twisting the ends back toward each other so the ends of the ring are flush.

 Repeat to add any additional buckles or clips.

HELPFUL HINTS

If your dress clips or buckles do not have holes for the jump rings, you can make your own. Use a small drill bit and handheld drill to carefully drill a hole in the metal of the piece. Be sure to wear safety goggles and place a piece of scrap wood underneath to protect your work surface.

4 Finish the necklace by using a jump ring to attach a clasp to one end of the chain.

SEQUIN BAUBLE
necklace

For a festive show-stopper necklace, take this easy DIY statement piece for a spin! It's guaranteed to sparkle, so pair this necklace with your favorite party dress for any holiday soirees. Because light Styrofoam balls form the sequin beads, you won't need to worry about being weighed down by heavy jewelry. Making the necklace is incredibly easy, and it comes together in about 45 minutes (plus drying time), so it's an ideal craft accompaniment for holiday movies to get you in the spirit of the season.

materials

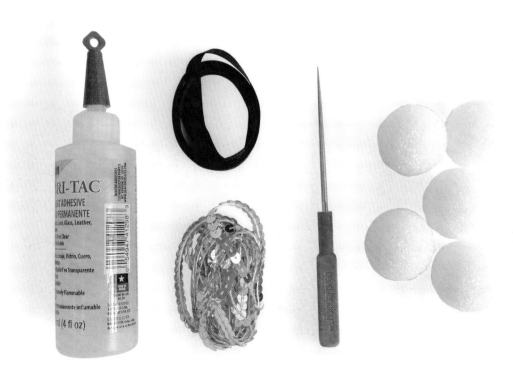

- Bead reamer or awl
- 5 1½ inch Styrofoam craft balls
- Fabric glue
- 8 feet of sequin trim
- Scissors
- 36 inches of ½-inch ribbon

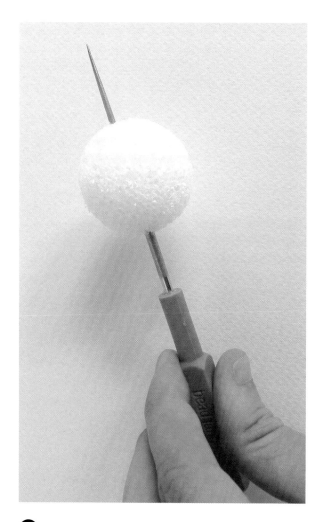

① Push the bead reamer or awl through the center of a Styrofoam ball. Repeat on the opposite side of the ball, going through the hole you just made, to widen the hole.

② Apply the glue around the top hole and halfway down the ball.

••● Make It Yours! ●••

For a twist on this necklace, buy assorted sizes of Styrofoam balls. You can try alternating or graduating sizes, with a large center ball and progressively smaller balls on the outside of the necklace.

3 Wrap the sequin trim around the ball, pressing into the glue and spiraling downward.

4 Add more glue to continue applying the sequin trim around the other end of the ball. Cut the trim and let dry according to package instructions. Repeat to make the other sequin balls.

5 Once the glue has dried, use the bead reamer or awl to push the end of the ribbon through the holes of a sequin ball.

6 Add the other balls to the ribbon. Trim the ribbon ends and tie in a bow to wear.

GOLD TUBE
necklace

$\mathcal{S}$ome of the best things come in threes, like the curved tubes of this modern necklace! In this DIY project, arced gold tubes stack together for a simple but sophisticated necklace. Ready for a date night or an evening out with the girls, this gold tube necklace is the perfect accompaniment to your favorite blouse or cocktail dress.

materials

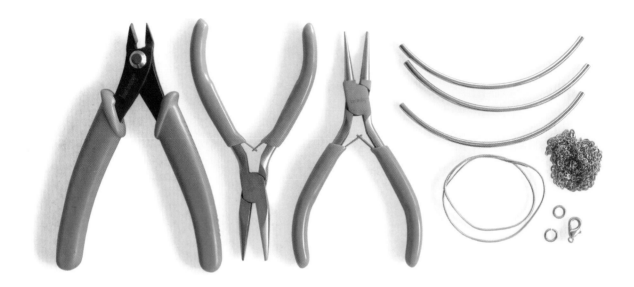

- 18 inches of gold craft wire
- 3 3mm × 100mm gold tubes
- Chain-nose jewelry pliers
- Round-nose jewelry pliers

- Wire cutters
- 48 inches of thin gold chain, cut into two 7½-inch, two 8-inch, and two 8½-inch pieces
- 2 7mm jump rings

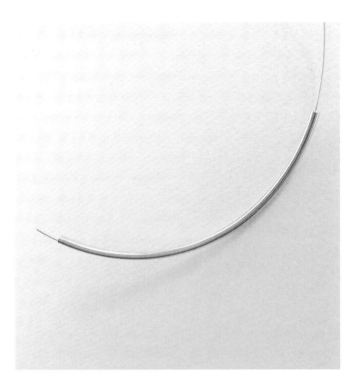

1 Slide the craft wire through one of the gold tubes.

STATEMENT NECKLACE SUPPLIES

You can buy gold tube beads of different sizes from brick-and-mortar and online bead stores, but thin copper tubing from the hardware store or large craft stores, cut to size, works as well.

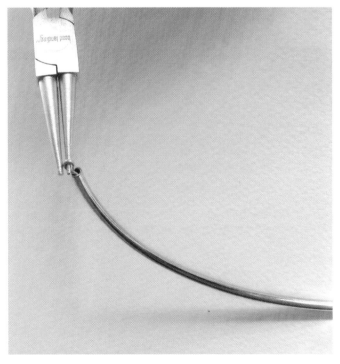

2 Bend the end of the wire into a small loop with the pliers, leaving partially open.

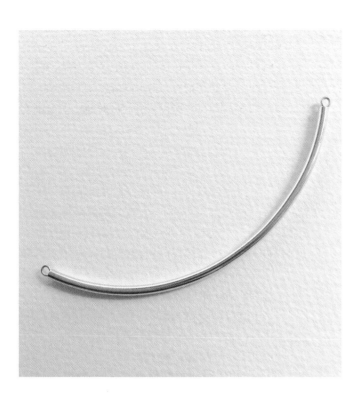

3 Clip the wire on the other side of the tube, leaving ½ inch. Bend this wire into a second loop.

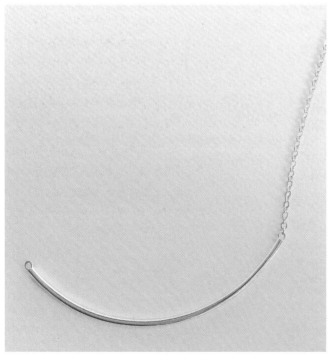

4 Attach the ends of each 7½-inch piece of chain to either of the wire loops, and close the loops with the round-nose pliers.

5 Repeat previous steps to add wire and loops to the other tubes. Attach the 8-inch chains to the second tube and the 8½-inch chains to the last tube.

6 Finally, open your jump rings by using two sets of pliers to grab on either side of the seam in the rings. Twist the pliers and ends of the jump rings away from each other in a north-south motion. Attach the jump rings to the ends of the chains, adding a clasp to one side, then close each ring by twisting the ends back toward each other so the ends of the ring are flush.

Appendix
SOURCES FOR MATERIALS

All the supplies for the statement necklaces in this book are listed in each tutorial, with measurements and sizes for materials that you can adjust to your own preferences. For ideas on where to buy supplies, use this guide of shops and online stores. However, don't feel limited by this list, because many great necklaces feature materials from the hardware store, thrift shop, dollar store, or even your own house!

Craft and Trimming Stores

A do-it-yourselfer can feel like a kid in a candy store wandering the aisles of one of these crafty destinations, so let your imagination run wild while browsing their selection—inspiration might be around the corner! Additionally, branch out of the jewelry section when looking for supplies. The materials for your next statement necklace could be amid the buttons, floral arrangements, or even kids' craft supplies!

MICHAELS

www.michaels.com for online store and retail locations
Find beads, chain, jewelry findings, and every other craft supply you'll need at this nationwide chain.

A.C. MOORE

www.acmoore.com for store locations
Located throughout the eastern United States, this arts and crafts store carries everything for your DIY needs.

JO-ANN FABRIC AND CRAFT STORES

www.joann.com for online store and retail locations

In addition to supplies for jewelry-making, Jo-Ann carries a great selection of trims and upholstery materials, such as cord and rope.

M&J TRIMMING

1008 6th Avenue, New York, NY 10018 and *www.mjtrim.com*

This Manhattan-based trim supply stocks every kind of trim or embellishment you could need. The brick-and-mortar store is worth a visit if you ever make it to NYC. While their online store has a smaller selection, it's great for basics, such as large-link chain.

Online Stores

Online shopping has made it possible for crafters to have access to all sorts of new materials from across the globe. Some supplies can go by different names, so when searching online, be flexible in your search terms. What one person calls a "faceted" bead might be called a "geometric" bead by another. Also, pay close attention to the measurements and sizes to ensure you're getting exactly what you want.

AMAZON

www.amazon.com

This online mega-retailer carries craft and jewelry-making supplies, streamlining your shopping cart.

EBAY

www.ebay.com

There's so much more to this website than just online auctions—such as buying in bulk or tracking down supplies you can't find in stores.

ETSY

www.etsy.com

For hard-to-find supplies, turn to Etsy's marketplace of vendors for exactly what you need. Etsy makes it easy for sellers from all over the world to share their goods.

STUDSANDSPIKES

www.studsandspikes.com

As their name suggests, this store is the go-to for any studs and spikes you might need, with a wide variety of styles for your projects.

Bead Stores

Many cities have small independent bead stores, a great place to find supplies, inspiration, and help in learning jewelry techniques. While it's great to support local businesses, if you don't have one in your community or can't find what you are looking for, try one of these online stores for jewelry-making supplies—findings, chain, beads, wire, and more.

BEADAHOLIQUE

www.beadaholique.com

GOODYBEADS

www.goodybeads.com

FIRE MOUNTAIN GEMS AND BEADS

www.firemountaingems.com

FUSIONBEADS

www.fusionbeads.com

Index

y

z

ABOUT THE AUTHOR

Erin Pruckno is a lifelong learner and crafter who grew up in a family of do-it-yourselfers and loves a great jewelry-making project. Teaching by day while crafting and blogging by night, Erin shares do-it-yourself tutorials and crafty inspirations on her website, *www.thanksimadeitblog.com.*